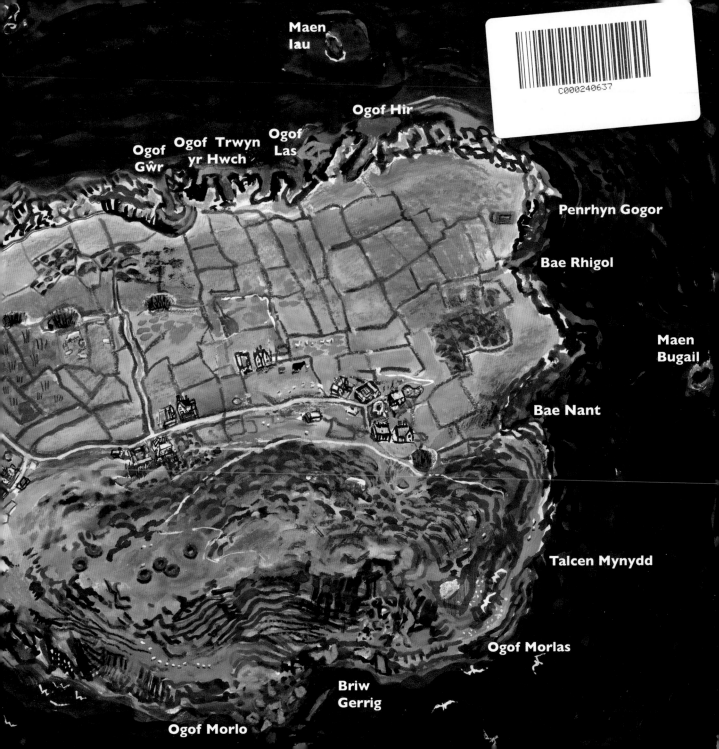

bardsey

bardsey

Essays by Christine Evans

Photographs by Wolf Marloh

Gomer

In memory of Wil and Nellie

CE

to Pempem

WM

Published in 2008 by Gomer Press, Llandysul, Ceredigion SA44 4JL
www.gomer.co.uk

ISBN 978 1 84323 819 5

A CIP record for this title is available from the British Library

This book is published with the financial support of the Welsh Books Council.

Printed and bound in Wales at Gomer Press, Llandysul, Ceredigion

contents

introduction

As I write, the January wind is howling. Just in from a walk on the headland, rubbing my hair dry, face still stinging, my mind is seething with images of the wild weather up there, where froth is being whipped from a dark sea and spiralling foam bounces up on to the land light as fleece, drying as salt-white dribbles on the turf. Nothing moves of its own volition: even sheep and birds are crouched in whatever shelter they can find. Across the Sound, the island is almost drowned in waves of blown mist, rain and spray. It reminds me of an image from medieval Welsh poetry. Bleddyn Fardd imagined winter swell relentless round Bardsey:

neud uchel gwendon gwyndir Enlli

white waves make loud the holy land of Enlli.

Simple statement as it is, the line contains both a sense of longing for the inaccessible place, and wonder rising out of myth about its specialness, its 'whiteness', or purity. It pictures the island almost as if flying over it, seeing it whole, fringed by besieging sea and storm, but holding steady in the flux and chaos.

In Welsh, *ynys yn y llif,* island in the flood-tide; in English, or rather Norse, Bardr's Island, the place has been lived on almost continuously through recorded history, and visited, at least, for thousands of years before that, as worked flints from the Mesolithic and Bronze Age cremations testify. It's a fragment of land at the edge, first landfall after the Irish Sea.

It is four decades since I saw Bardsey for the first time. I came for a week in 1968, stayed for three, and have spent every summer there since. This book is an attempt to share the island and some of its stories with people who are not so privileged.

at first sight

Arrival

A long hot day on the shingle beach at Porth Meudwy, 'the hermit's harbour'. One by one, paddling children were herded towards lunch in caravan or holiday cottage, the last swimmer disappeared behind the boathouse, towelled himself vigorously, and set off at a trot up the cliff path towards Aberdaron. A few lobster boats came in, small traditional clinker-built craft; the fishermen glanced uncuriously at me, unloaded their catch and petrol cans and a smashed creel or two into vans that had seen better days, and puttered off up the cart-track. Slowly dust settled, gulls resumed their patient stations on the shining water. Mid-July, basking weather under a clear sky, and I was alone by the whispering sea.

I had been summoned by Miss Averilda Williams, 'Willikitch', cookery teacher at the grammar school in Pwllheli, where I had just finished my first year. When she had told me of the island where she spent the entire summer holidays, I'd made interested noises but with no serious intention of taking up her casual invitation to stay with her and her black cocker spaniel. After industrial West Yorkshire and then a couple of years living over a High Street butcher's at the end of the Tube line, I was looking forward to exploring the beaches and sleepy villages of Llŷn with a swimming costume and a picnic in the boot of my old Morris 1,000. But, a week or so after the end of term, a letter without any address except 'Enlli' gave me little option: 'Expect you next Saturday 16th. Boat won't leave before 12. Bring plenty of old clothes for painting, and a cake.'

9

Painting? I supposed she needed help renovating the old farmhouse she'd spoken of, whose walls were always peeling with damp. With little enthusiasm I bought a used kit-bag at the Army and Navy Stores, and a jam and cream sponge from the Co-op. That was my idea of a good tea in those days; I hadn't yet observed the 'two kinds of cake and a scone' rule of Llŷn farm-wives.

I knew nothing of Bardsey. I had read about islands, of course, when I was much younger: Enid Blyton had prepared me to expect puffins among sea-pinks, as well as smugglers – always bearded, to indicate their rascally black natures – and a wrecked schooner or two, and Ronald Lockley had written of talking goats and ponies in *Early Morning Island*, an account of life on Skokholm through the eyes of his daughter. I didn't have time to read up about the history of pilgrimage and the twenty thousand saints supposed to be buried on 'wonderful Enlli', as Rilda invariably referred to it. I did explore as far as the cove where the boat would pick me up, but didn't know to drive to the end of the peninsula to see where I was heading: sitting on the beach, I looked out at the two rocky islets out in the bay and wondered if one of them could be Bardsey. It looked like being a dull week.

As the afternoon wore on, and I got hungrier and thirstier, I was reassured by the slow gathering of other passengers. There was a tentative approach, a shy exchange of information. Three skinny young men with oversized, lumpy rucksacks and binoculars were going to the Bird Observatory; a family arrived trundling a wheelbarrow full of babies and cardboard boxes spilling packets of rice and digestive biscuits; a serenely smiling middle-aged couple with an aged golden retriever settled themselves in a patch of shade.

At last, well after four o'clock, a large open boat smartly painted in red and white throbbed its way round the point, and a dinghy was propelled rapidly towards the beach by a young man standing in the bow and waggling a single oar from side to side. I had never seen anyone sculling before: it seemed both ingenious and more natural than rowing. The little boat skimmed the surface and in a moment its four or five passengers sprang ashore. All were men, wearing denim fishermen's smocks, and almost all had beards; thick, vigorous growths of hair that gave them a strong, stocky look. They were quick and intent, carrying the dinghy beyond the tide-line and unloading mail bags, a sack that bulged and crowed, cardboard boxes marked 'Wyau' (eggs) and such. They seemed to be taking no interest in us, the respectfully diffident assemblage. When one of them began whirring the starter of a battered van parked near the stone storehouse, I couldn't bear the uncertainty – or the increasing need to sit tightly cross-legged. I had to know if this was indeed the boat for Bardsey, and when it might be setting off. Staunchly I approached the boatman. His beard was gingery, I noticed, and well-trimmed; definitely not smuggler-like. Nor were the spectacles, the tumble of sun-bleached hair, the serious brown eyes.

'Pushy' was how my enquiry came across, I was told later. It resulted in a level look and a carefully informative reply about fuel and stores being more important than holiday timetables. 'We go when we're ready, as soon as we can.' So I had time to walk back up the little steep-sided valley, sniffing the honeysuckle and listening to the birds in a wonderfully private spot beside the stream before we were eventually loaded and off.

Once round Aberdaron Point the long wait and the ignominy of getting aboard (I had never been in a boat before and tumbled in bum first) began to seem worthwhile. There was the place, further than I had imagined, a low humped shape that reminded me of the simile in *Paradise Lost* about the 'night-founder'd' fisherman who camped on the back of a slumbering whale, thinking it a safe island anchorage. There was the swelling curved bulk of Leviathan's back, dark and apparently streamlined, sloping down to the suggestion of a head underwater. More than a physical resemblance, though, was the surprise of it, a sense of encounter. It seemed to be waiting, I thought; but as though, at any moment, the island could let go of its moorings and drift over the horizon, like a great sea-beast resuming its migration to deep ocean.

And then we were out in the open sea, salt on the lips, and a flicker of iridescence in the spray. The water was variations of grey, not the uniform blue of postcards: there was deep green of depth in it, and dark streaks that were almost purple. We pushed across long slicks of tide, even on such a calm day, and slid over glinting patches like mirrors of smoked glass. Such deceitful smoothness would be encircled by rougher water, where the surface was lumpy, goosefleshed by swift, contradictory currents, whirlpools and mysterious upwellings of energy.

Slowly the island grew, as though it were pulling us towards it on underwater strings. Between us and its dark hump, a line of birds lifted into the air, late sun snagging on white wing-tips, as though they were signalling us in. The steep sweep was coming into focus, fractured and fissured into a pattern of shadows broken up by the fawns and greens of vegetation. A richer green, bracken flowed like water around an earthslip that had ripped a bald patch below the summit and where giant boulders lay tumbled, still bare of growth. The boat seemed suddenly to pick up speed, gliding past sheer rock walls where sea-birds perched and called. A month earlier, the birdwatcher sitting next to me shouted, the ledges would have been stacked with guillemots and razorbills, but the chicks had fledged and most had gone back to sea. He nudged binoculars at me, pointing out a fulmar riding an updraught without moving a muscle, and named the kittiwakes' insistent melancholy cries.

Someone was standing like a sentinel, dark against the skyline, as we passed under a high crag that jutted out in the shape of a raven's beak. A stone's throw from the rocks now, we were close enough to see the patterns and scratches on them above a tide-line of black, spiky algae – but still there seemed no way in. And then the boat swept with the current into the bay, and the island's real face was revealed. It seemed to open its arms in welcome, grey stone farmhouses drowsing in late sun, a lap of soft green fields, the red and white stripes of the lighthouse startlingly bright.

A small group of people were waiting beside the tractor and trailer on the slipway. A pigtailed child was paddling, net in hand. She watched us land without interest or concern while a smaller red-haired boy scarcely looked up from lifting hanks of seaweed to peer into the rock-pools beneath. Unloading and hauling the boat up beyond the reach of the tide was accomplished in minutes, men and women moving easily, with the grace of being sure of what they were doing, of being in place. Apart from their jeans and denim fishermen's smocks, the children's shorts and tee shirts, they might have been from any period in history. The young man I'd spoken to – who had steered the boat – swung up on to the tractor. 'Ride if you like, you can unload your luggage.' The evening sky was huge, the air warm and gentle as we were bumped along with the luggage on the back of the trailer, past a field with hay in stacks and another where a red cow standing over a tiny black calf looked up reprovingly at our noise. It was like an illustration from a child's picture book. The little girl rode standing up at the front, thick brown hair escaping from its plaits to fly in a halo round her head. All the way up the track, stopping to offload at each grey stone farmhouse, I was enchanted.

I went up to bed in the room next to the ruins and the graveyard with my head teeming with images of the day and the journey and the arrival. When I blew out the candle, blackness surged back, padding the edges of everything, absorbing all sound and muffling thought. I slept instantly, and so heavily that when I was woken hours later by gasping screams, it took me long moments to remember where I was. Nant lies tucked under the shoulder of the mountain, at the north end of the island, and I had been warned at supper about the thousands of birds – Manx shearwaters – which came in from the sea at night. But these were like no other bird-calls I had ever heard; they were disconcertingly like the cries of deranged humanity. An asthmatic war-whoop was abruptly choked off into throaty gurgles; an uncoordinated chorus of cackles whispered hoarsely just above me; a distant drunken multitude were yelling, over and over, the name of their team – *Bardsey Ro-ow-vers, Bardsey Row – vers, Bardsey Rooo* . . . As fast as they ran out of breath, another mob took up the chant and flew with it, like a round, endlessly.

The night was thick, I saw, sliding open the window and leaning out into the clogged air. No trace of lighthouse beams now: bringing my bag up earlier, I had watched the loom of them illuminating the room, a regular flash lightening walls and ceiling. The heat of the day had given way to fog. No wonder it had been so dark when I came to bed. And as I thought this, I heard a double droning mutter that must be the fog-horn, so faint it might have been miles away or buried at the bottom of the sea.

I hung there, listening for it to come again, and when it did, it seemed to stimulate a new frenzy of shrieks. Nothing to see, however hard I peered, even when an individual bird, gulping and screeching, passed so low over the roof that its labouring wing-beats thumped the air like heart-beats in panic. Apparently nobody but myself was disturbed by the din; there was no one else awake to witness the pulsing energy of these countless unseen beings. I climbed back into the high bed and lay in the dark, washed by urgent calls of need and finding until sleep floated me away once more.

On the mountain

By morning the mist had thinned to white breath stretched in swirls across the high sky, polishing my Wellingtons and glistening on each blade of grass and bracken frond as I pushed through them towards the top of the mountain.

First thing, I had been sent to fetch milk and butter from Rilda's cold store – a basin of rock where fresh water overflowing from the well dripped and pooled. A white enamel bucket, its lid weighted with a big stone, stood shaded by ferns in the brimming water and kept its contents as cool as if they had been in a fridge. After breakfast, I followed the narrow footpath that skirted the pool and its small stream to where it divided – one arm going behind the chapel and up to the highest point in a series of gentle zigzags, the other climbing more steeply to round the rocky north-west corner. This was the wilder option. I took it, turning left and trampling smells of water-mint in the long wet grass, then wild thyme higher and drier, until my stride became a scramble over granite outcrops sticking up out of the bracken like skerries in a green flood. In the middle of one waist-high patch, a boulder where I rested was not only spattered with bright gold lichen but had its own integral sparkle of crystal speckles. Other stones were reddish or creamy-streaked. Three choughs were carving airy arcs above, wings spread to the fingertips for delicate balance. I recalled a Cornish legend in which King Arthur does not die but is transformed into a chough, the red-legged crow, so that he will never leave his beloved coast. Losing height, the birds rollercoasted over me, as if it were a special display, tumbling together before one veered off over the hill, screaming its name the way it used to be pronounced: *Chee-ow, chee-ow*, with the rapture of a small boy in racing-car mode.

Then there was only quiet, not even any sheep calls; only my even steps and snatches of bee-song as I squeezed through a gorse thicket in flower. Suddenly I was standing on a wide shelf of rock I recognised as limestone, pitted here and there with sockets brimming with water that reflected the sky. The grass here was fine as on a moorland, and between cushions of thrift, the sea-pink flowers dry and papery brown now, the ground was almost shockingly bare, like bone glimpsed through a thin covering of hair. A great brow of rock faced out over the Sound to the long grey-blue line of mainland hills two miles away. When I eventually learned its name it was with a frisson of recognition: *Talcen y Mynydd* means either (or both) the 'gable-end of the mountain' and its forehead. But I was on a firm path that led away from the cliff, down and round, under a smaller overhang and into another sort of place – a glade? No, there would have to be trees to call it that. Childhood reading offered me the word *dell*, thickly carpeted with lush grass and the duller green of bluebell leaves. The air that danced off the sea was clean and bright, the rock wall curving at the back had soaked up hours of sun. I lay back in a drowse of sea-shift and cloud-sway for several of those delicious moments of unfocus when time has no meaning. Perhaps I was contemplating, as I have often since at that spot, how the sight of the distant mainland emphasises a sense of remoteness.

I must have been very still, for when a sudden scuffling movement prompted me to sit up, it was to see the grey-brown back and white scut of a rabbit retreating along the path. Presumably, going about its business from one neatly-nibbled patch to another, it had startled itself by almost falling over me. For all I knew there might have been a whole family of them coming to peer at a human harmless in semi-conscious state. Getting to my feet I realised that for a while there had been a steadily increasing background noise: a pervasive, hectoring hubbub as if somewhere just out of sight a busy market was doing a roaring trade.

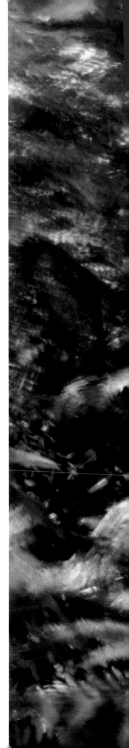

Round the corner, the path rose steeply away from the sea. There was a teetering moment of stepping across a crumbling bit, and then I was looking out over a slope crowded with gulls heckling and jostling for space among grass as improbably green as the illustrations on packets of lawn fertiliser. Plenty of nitrogenous manure, then, and a distinctively fishy smell in the air. Perhaps not wafting up from the gull colony, for right at my feet and all around were holes. The whole slope was spongy and undermined, a tenement of burrows, each entrance marked with a tell-tale white splash of guano. These were the homes my night-visitors had been seeking so urgently. Over breakfast I had been instructed in the ways of the Manx shearwater, and now sat wondering at an instinct so strong it could draw a bird back from the South Atlantic to the same burrow and the same mate year after year; that could make creatures perfectly at ease in two elements – air and water – risk themselves, shuffling about on land for half a year to raise a single chick. I lay down with my ear against warm earth, but could hear nothing. Some of these burrows must be occupied, must be sheltering a parent bird sitting tight on its white egg, or a chick dozing away the daylight until its next feed of sand-eels or sprats. Tentatively I reached inside the nearest hole – almost up to the elbow, fingers ready to flinch at first touch of feathers or an egg's smoothness – but only once, then I lost my nerve. 'A nasty bite,' I'd been told. 'Beak like a pair of pliers, and sharp.'

All the way up the steep pull to the top I could see holes facing seawards, each with its little trodden-down balcony in front like holiday flats, and I thought of the young birds emerging at the end of summer to look out at the stars, as Rilda had described, learning the patterns of the constellations so they might, after six or seven years on the wing, find their way back to this safe bit of land to breed.

On the rocky spine of the island that fell away on both sides, I was at once tiny, dwarfed by sea and sky, and triumphant – king of the castle. The ridge was that crystalline white limestone again, sharpnesses gleaming like shards of bone as they caught the sun. And here *were* bones: first one cross of black feathers lying in the heather, then another. Just wing feathers, wrenched off the body and discarded, a whole scattering of them. It struck me that they resembled the short black capes priests sometimes wear, called scapulars because they just cover the shoulder blades. Strangely appropriate on this old monks' island. I touched the nearest one, and opened the wings like a fan. They flexed smoothly, each feather silky smooth and lustrous black. It was clean, with hardly a sign of the force which had torn the bird apart, only a ripped knot of muscle ragged at what would be the armpit. This, then, was why the shearwaters waited for thick dark before returning to their bunkers. These were some who hadn't made it, or whose mates had returned too late for them to get out to sea before daylight. They had been picked off by opportunists, as all such predators must be, I supposed; fellow birds, too, for I'd heard before coming of the island's lack of other suspects. No snakes, of course, on a holy island (like Ireland) but no foxes, badgers, polecats or moles into the bargain. And most fortunate of all, especially for the ground-nesting birds, no rats.

A few yards away, a fulmar floated calmly past, wings held out stiffly at full stretch, surfing effortlessly on thin air. Its eye was level with mine but if its glance flicked over me I was of no more significance than a fellow traveller on the Tube. And for an instant there was that dizzy sense of not knowing which of us was moving forward, which standing still and merely watching. Then it was past and there was just bright air and the whole long coast-line of Cardigan Bay, the old volcanoes of Llŷn and the Snowdon ridge hazy with distance.

I moved closer to the edge, the scree and dizzy tumble of the east side drawing my gaze. So many different rocks, heaped up into a pile when the ancient sea-bed first split and heaved. To my left the bulge of dirty white stone like the boss of an immense round shield held out over the void; immediately below that a long scatter of boulders, some the size and shape of small cars, caught and held in the moment of falling. Beyond them, where huge black slabs were piled at the water's edge, the small dark head of a seal created a wake as it moved steadily away from the island, having emerged perhaps from the cave that my birdwatcher guide had pointed out from the boat. A ewe picked her way purposefully along the lowest of three narrow paths above the sea. As she disappeared behind an overhang, twin lambs came into view, racing to

catch up and unable to resist kicking up their heels and giving little bucks of exuberance as though it were a level field, rather than the edge of a precipice.

The gull clamour was left behind now and the other birds were quiet, in their mid-morning drowse. The sea was calm, shining with benevolence on this side; on the west, though, to my right, it was ruffled and grey, with long lines of white foam around Carreg Rhona (the seal rock) and the ragged shore-line. A small dark blue boat rode the swell, a fisherman in yellow oilskin coat standing in the stern, braced against the rock and surge of the waves. I wished I had binoculars.

Foxgloves clustered round the cairn on the highest point of the mountain, leaning out over the edge and swaying like rockets waiting to be lit and shoot in magenta arcs across the sea. There were nettles too, I found, hidden in the bracken. I was once told that where they grew had often been a place of human habitation but this seemed an unlikely spot, exposed as it was. Perhaps people thousands of years ago had been less soft than us, or more in need of watching for raiders, for this was a superb vantage point – north, far into Llŷn; south and east, the whole long line of Cardigan Bay; and west, where the Irish hills could be glimpsed at nightfall as a line of grey tents on the horizon. For a moment images of the older island hovered in my imagination: below me, not the tidy patchwork of fields but a tangle of scrub (hazel, willow, stunted oak) and marshland, and Viking sails instead of the long grey coaster far out there, making passage so slowly it seemed to hang a third of the way down from the skyline.

The going now was easy, the path undulating broad as a saddle and widening to greensward, and the southern part of the island, the wiggly bit of the tadpole's tail, spread itself out before me like a growing map. Its irregular pattern of fields in different shades of green was pleasing to the eye – hedge-banks and the track winding between dark strips of meadow or tidy bleached squares where the hay had been harvested. In the furthest one, three figures with long rakes or forks were moving steadily down the rows of haycocks, and as I watched, they started tossing the grass and spreading it to dry.

There was a patch of scrub and a pond like a glittering eye, a stream meandering down to the sea and half a dozen cattle in the shade of a big white rock – I guessed there might be a spring there too – but the farmhouses tucked in the shelter of the hill were hidden, under the ridge. The little stone-built boat shed at the landing place stood out clearly, with the red and white of the boat peeping out round it, just where the island began to narrow between twin curves of sea. The tide was high, filling the east bay right up to the rocks and shingle of its beach, and threatening to cover the white shell-sand of the western shore. Pinched like a Victorian girl's waist, the land became a bridge to a southern promontory with the lighthouse planted stolid and four-square in the middle of it. I had not known there were square lighthouses before, and wondered if this week I might find out more about it. The two men – the keepers – who had walked down to the boat to collect their mail and cigarettes (and maybe to look over any newcomers) had seemed friendly enough. I could ask Rilda, and perhaps tomorrow explore the rocky coves down there.

For today, it was enough, and I wanted to get back. I hadn't really got my bearings or settled in at Nant yet. It had been gathering dark when we'd finally arrived at the furthest house from the harbour, and in the slight awkwardness of greeting people I didn't know and with whom I was to spend a week, I hadn't liked to look around too much. All I'd noticed was a huge stone cross and a roofless ruin like a broken tooth right outside the room where we'd had breakfast. There were things to discover there too. And I was startlingly hungry.

Meetings

After a couple of false starts involving plunges into gullies flooded by bracken and getting caught in gorse and bramble entanglements, a long zigzag path presented itself. It led me steeply down over a stone stile on to the main track opposite the big house where the smiling couple had unloaded their considerable baggage, including bags of cement, a ladder and a lot of planks. The woman, Gwen, called a greeting over the garden wall and invited me in for coffee. 'But we're in a bit of a mess, got part of the floor up in the hall – wet rot, you see' – so I declined and tramped north. By now, out of the breeze, it was really hot.

Like all routes created by feet rather than machines, this road follows the lie of the land, dipping and bending, in places narrow and stony as a goat track, in others a wide grassy lane between stone walls. Whereas up on top I'd experienced a sense of limitless space, as though the bubble of my consciousness could expand, here I was an ant crawling along the belly of the island, the bulk of the hill on my right and sticky heat pressing me into insignificance. But I was not alone: other ants were scurrying, with more purpose. The wheelbarrow was in use again. It approached and passed, loaded now for a day on the beach, the baby peering out over her mother's shoulder, the two bigger ones toddling behind with their spades. Radio music spilling out of a small cottage – the only traditional Welsh cottage I'd seen on the island – and the smell of frying bacon, a chair pulled into the open doorway, testified to a lazy Sunday morning. Next came a roofless ruin beside the track, where the children I'd met on the beach were intent on a game involving crumbling the flowers of red dock and poking the ruined fireplace with a gorse stick. 'This is Mrs Dog's house,' the little girl announced in answer to my hello, 'and we're making tea.' She was about five, so serious she was frowning a little; her brother younger, with a friendly unfocused grin.

On and up and past the turning to the chapel and its minister's house set back rather importantly, past the imposing granite walls that enclosed each farmyard and gave shelter from the salt wind, past the iron gates that gave access up three steps to all that was left of the Abbey, a square tower open to the sky, its windows jagged wounds in the crumbling sandstone walls, each block thickly encrusted with grey-green lichen. Scattered among the grass around it were headstones, one of white marble, five or six of the big slate boxes so popular with the Victorian bereaved, and stumps of rock marking older graves as well as two tall Celtic crosses – the cross enclosed in a circle.

'It represents eternity. Time and eternity meet in Our Lord's suffering, do you see.'

A grey-haired woman had come up silently behind me. 'And you see the inscription? *Respect the twenty thousand saints buried on or near this spot.* Wonderful, isn't it? *Nihil ad vos? O viatores omnes.* Brenda loved that, the idea that we are all pilgrims whether we know it or not . . . You'll have read *Tide-race*, of course?'

Then, with a change of tone, a sort of pinning-down satisfaction, 'You're staying with Rilda, aren't you? I saw you go past last night. I'm Eva, I'm just back from a year in India. Teachers are so desperately needed there, I'll tell you about it. Come and have a cup of tea one day . . .'

She led me to the next walled enclosure where the gigantic stone cross loomed in solitary splendour, telling me that it was a memorial to the owner of the island who, a hundred years before, had spent a fortune on new houses and farm buildings. Lord Newborough visited the island often, his son too, staying at Plas Bach where rooms were always kept ready for them. It was on his instructions that the zigzag path was made to the top of the mountain and his last wish was to be buried in the graveyard. 'And there he is, down there!' pointing to a metal grille set in the ground before the monument. 'In a lead coffin in a sealed vault. Of course, we all sleep on top of bones here. Some people find it spooky, but I don't listen to silly stories.'

There were two other house guests at Nant, and by the time I stepped into the cool shade of the thick-walled house, they were all sitting down to lunch. I was glad to join them, glad, too, that it had been felt too hot for a traditional roast dinner with rice pudding, and assured Rilda that homemade bread and cheese was just right. Afterwards I described where I had walked and how delightful it had been, trying to show belated gratitude for the chance to come and stay. Sophie, a gentle old lady from Llandudno, was almost blind, and I tried to describe the birds and scenery in some detail for her. David – the fifteen-year-old nephew of a vicar friend – was interested only in getting out to catch the best tide for fishing. Rilda wanted to know who I had seen, and what they were doing, and she enjoyed identifying them for me. 'That's Gwen Robson, she's been coming to stay since she was a girl and now she has a lease on Plas and spends every minute she can here. But the house is in a terrible state, it was half-wrecked by a hermit who went off his head. I'll tell you sometime. Quakers, good people, not afraid of hard work.'

Carreg Bach, the cottage, was where George Evans, the warden of the Observatory, lived with his wife Fran who was visiting her mother just now. The playing children

belonged to the farm at Tŷ Nesaf. 'English, but very nice. From the West Country, came when the children were babies. Bright, but they need to go to school. Mary has a wonderful garden, I was going to ask you to pop down and ask her for some vegetables. Mind the sheep-dog, though.'

Twelve people lived on the island all the year round, apparently, and that number trebled in summer. Wiping the sink, Rilda talked of Wil and Nellie down the island at Tŷ Pella. 'They say it's called that because it's the farthest house from the Abbey and where the monks used to land. It's the main farm, of course; I don't like to think what'll happen when Wil retires; he's talking about it. They've been here over forty years, but Ernest their son prefers the sea. He won't take over the farm, I don't think.'

When it was time for tea, which the women seemed to know instinctively (I was amazed that anyone still sat down to bread and butter and jam in the middle of the afternoon; among friends of my generation it seemed quaint as tiffin), my Co-op sponge was put on a doily on a plate in the middle of the table. It wasn't improved by its day in the kit-bag, and then being tossed from boat to boat had squashed it considerably, but Rilda – a cookery teacher with a formidable reputation! – was generous. She ate a slice valiantly. 'Not bad,' she pronounced, 'for a *shop* cake. And tomorrow you can make a real one.'

'It's Monday tomorrow. She'll have to come down to the Cafn to see the lobsters being packed.' David, too, had appeared just as the kettle boiled and was eating steadily through the cake. He'd brought a strong smell of rather old seaweed and three wrasse, two bony bronze ones and a third amazingly colourful fish – green and gold, with a touch of turquoise on the lips – that Rilda said was a cuckoo wrasse, and please to leave them all outside for her to deal with.

'I've never seen a lobster. But I must do something to help Rilda too.'

'You're here to enjoy the island. They won't be loading up till after *cinio*. You go off up the mountain tomorrow, and take a blanket and a book, and have a rest. That's what I do.'

If it was, there was no sign of it. She was busy from early morning till night, cooking and looking after us all and preparing the house next door for a big group of young church people the following week, and when she wasn't carrying mattresses out to air in the sun, or scrubbing stairs or polishing windows, she was filling tins with fruit cakes and flapjacks in readiness. She had got Hendy, the twin house next door, designated as a church hostel, and after years of neglect, had spruced it up and equipped it with enough metal bedsteads, horsehair mattresses and coarse ex-army blankets for nine sleepers. The pantry shelves were piled with catering-sized tins and pans, scrounged from school kitchens. The painting had all been done; she showed me the *tŷ bach*, the little stone-built privy in the garden, freshly distempered in pure white. 'Makes it smell a bit better,' she mouthed, as if voicing an indelicacy. I looked at the not very capacious bucket, and wondered. Forty people were expected, some to sleep in tents or in Tŷ Capel across the field. I was glad it was not my problem; it had been agreed that I could make up beds and sort out candles.

I slipped out next morning before anyone else was up and cut across the fields behind the house. They fell steeply to the sea in a long green valley bordered by willows, hops and wild plums within the walls of an old garden. The trees were already heavy with round fruit, still very green, and I could see there'd be a good harvest of blackberries in a few weeks if the birds didn't get them. The bushes and long grass were alive with small brown birds hopping and chirping sibilantly, willow warblers at a guess. Some seemed to be grazing on tiny spiders picked off webs heavy with drops of dew.

I found myself in a wonderfully serene bay, narrow but deep, with flat slabs at the water's edge. This, I knew, was where Rilda said the monks had landed and where she came to swim almost daily, but the water was in shadow. It was clear but green with depth and not inviting; the sort of place where to imagine a drowned face rising silently, pale and blind. I shivered. The previous evening, having discovered that 'Brenda', the painter and writer Brenda Chamberlain, had lived in Carreg, I'd found *The Green Heart* in the bookcase in Nant and a grim image from a poem called 'Islandman' had clearly lodged in my imagination:

Lifting his lobster pots at sunrise,
He is not surprised when drowned sailors
Wearing ropes of pearl round green throats
Nod their heads at him from underwater forests.

I climbed the rocks back up into brightness and trod springy turf along an earth parapet where rabbits smug with sun could hardly bestir themselves to scuttle into the gorse. The day smelled wonderfully fresh. Sauntering beside the sparkling sea, I found myself singing a wordless tune.

Along the west

This coast was rugged and exposed, the rocks more eaten away and threatening, like the *blakke rokkes* in the Britanny of the *Franklin's Tale*. Big boulders like watching women blocked the way. The path scuttled and dodged along the very edge of the land, parts of it eroded away, usually on the trickiest bits, but there were no high cliffs here. It would be a tumble on to hard rock, not a fall headlong to the sea. On the tide-line of each gully I came to was a litter of bones, driftwood smashed to fragments and bits of plastic in indelible colours, and each had its resident oystercatchers warning me off, encircling me in shrill staccato: *'Keep! Keep! Keep!'* There must still be nestlings nearby, then, crouched for camouflage among the speckled pebbles. As I worked my way lower over the sharp rocks to avoid disturbing them the black head of a seal bobbed under and surfaced further out, letting nothing escape its serious stare. The tide was low, leaving rock-pools where tiny fish flicked and little crabs scuttled as my shadow fell across them. All the crannies were packed with shellfish: snail-like whelks, yellow and grey winkles clinging to each other in heaps as if ready for the fishmonger's stall, and limpets like calcified flowers stuck to the rocks.

On the shell-sand beach the tide was still retreating with long weary sighs, leaving a straggle of weed, shells and a scattering of other objects too. A dead (phew, long-dead) oystercatcher with its distinctive orange beak, still sharp enough to chisel limpets off rocks; a papery cluster of dog-whelk eggs, a couple of chalky ellipses that I recognised as cuttle-fish from when we had a budgie. And the human flotsam and jetsam: Coca-Cola cans, lobster pot floats, a massive twist of rope, a doll's shoe. A child's dress, washed off a beach somewhere while she was playing in the sand? More feathers, and a spray of yellow silk roses, only slightly faded. What was the story behind that?

The seal was still out there, watching. Or – maybe it was another; this one looked bigger, paler. As I looked, several seal heads emerged, and from the two islets out to sea came a long low howling moan, lugubrious in the extreme, more like a dog than any sea creature, I thought. All the same . . . seal-song. I screwed up my eyes and peered out towards the rocky skerries, as several more took up the tune.

Perhaps it signified a change in the weather. The sea was different today: it crawled and twitched like the skin of a huge animal asleep and dreaming of violence. The wind had got up from the west, too. David reported that there'd been talk down at Tŷ Pella of a low pressure system coming in: not good news for men who made their living in small boats, lobster fishing and ferrying people to the island. I had noticed the older man moving with rheumatic stiffness, letting his son do most of the heavy work. And they had all the farm-work too – they had not long finished shearing, wet weather had delayed the hay and soon the lambs would have to be rounded up, sorted and taken across to market.

I made my way inland from the restless glitter of water and, without any intention of doing so, lay down in a hollow that was a well of green warmth. There seemed something quite significant in that simple action, a freedom to obey natural instincts. 'When I was weary, I lay down.' The men and women who had lived and laboured here would probably never have allowed the idea to enter their heads, let alone just take time out. Sprawling luxuriously, watching the sky change as the tides of the air worked on it, I invoked a sense of all those who had gone before and whose patterns might somehow persist, breathed in as a mixture of sweetness and salt. Looking up at the mountain, toying with the idea of doing the walk in reverse from here, I found my mind full of images and words for them, and let them dance.

Walking the West, Early

Lie in the lap of the morning and
let light dance round you.
Stonechat chip-chipping at his flints.

At your back
the sense of watchers on the hill

(coracle and long-boat
doves tame to the hand, coneys
smug in a field of June oats
plainsong and the small blurred flutes
of willow warblers.)

Hear the tide turn stones over,
nudging them to shine, determined
as men bending to their creels, women
bowed down by buckets of water.

Watch warm air from beyond Wicklow
stroking the skin of the water
till it swells and lifts
tipped with silver

uncoiling intricate currents

scarfing its whirlpools
with silk, with miniature round mirrors
glittering lenses goggling you
from the bright strands below

the depths green as malachite
guileless as paint-water
(the green so hard to rinse out.)

Following the sheep path, your feet rolled
on sea-flung fistfuls of black beads
storm-smashed bladderwrack;

through the zigzag scribble
of oystercatcher cries, you had to work a way
round rock shattered into

incoherence, those gargling slits
and nightmare crouchings
with an odd sea-boot caught fast and a small pink dress
laid out as if to dry

and you glimpsed how each completed moment
seals itself like a quickened womb
shaping a sill for the next.

Now, gulls hector as you climb.
On their daylong ride, three chough scream
over shy blue pools
of vernal squill, their honey
fainter than bluebells', their sepals
tiny light-sipping stars

and over scapulars of stiff black feathers
picked of flesh and tossed aside
under the herring-gull's mad gorse eye.

The mainland twitches in its sleep.
The shadows all point forwards, to the sea.

Learning the Island

Over the next days, I began to appreciate how an island is the best place to recognise subtle changes in weather. On all but the calmest days, the slightest air movements can be felt and the sound of the sea, breathing, all around you is a living presence. Hear it change, look up and out to the west, and you can see storm-clouds or rainbows or the wispy cloud that foretells a fine tomorrow.

Monday morning was washing, not just following tradition but also because it was the day the fishermen went ashore to sell their catch of lobster and crab, and it was a matter of pride that they should be clean and tidy. I got back to Nant to find Rilda with a line full of laundry but muttering over David's jeans. She had pounded and rubbed them but the stains wouldn't shift. I was sent down to the farm for the milk and some eggs. 'And ask Nellie how she gets the men's clothes clean.'

'Tide,' was the answer, appropriately enough and readily given. 'Soak them overnight in Tide washing powder and then give them a good scrubbing on the washboard.' Nellie was a strong woman, no taller than me but stocky and immeasurably more powerful. I'd seen her swinging sacks of chicken feed and hoisting bottled gas cylinders out of the boat. Her forearms were thickly freckled below the short sleeves of her flowered blue blouse. She had a straight gaze, as though she had nothing to hide; she looked right at you with clear brown eyes. Her hair was pure white – snow-bright where the sunlight glanced on it as she moved between the windows in the low-roofed dairy. Huge earthenware crocks with slate lids stood in rows on low shelves. I breathed in a faint, clean, acid tang that reminded me of Caerphilly cheese and the yellow soap that used to be sold in blocks for rough work. *Sunlight*, it was called. Everything was scrubbed spotless, the grain of the table smooth and bleached, each pane in the low windows clear and shining. An empty stand dominated the centre of the shed. She saw my glance at it, and explained. The big churn and the cream separator had just been taken to her daughter's farm on the mainland. That year was the first that she had not made butter. For how long? Longer than she could remember; for years before she married she worked on farms and it was churning twice a week on some of them. She was trying to get used to the thin taste of shop-bought stuff, but it was putting her off eating bread. 'We're getting too old,' she said, straining the milk. 'It was a job, you know, skimming and ripening the cream and churning. People don't want it any more. Too much work just for us.' She poured the milk into the enamel can and settled the lid carefully so it wouldn't spill. '*Dyna chi*. Tell Rilda there'll be eggs tomorrow; I gave the last to John Bell from the lighthouse.'

There was quite a gathering at the landing place in the afternoon to watch the fishing boats, three of them, towing in the big wooden boxes they used to store a week's catch. Wire catches and rope ties were undone and the lids thrown back releasing a strong smell of ocean and fish. Inside was a slow heave of living creatures exposed to alien air and unfiltered light. Lobsters creaked and huddled, clacking their delicately-fringed indigo blue tails in warning or distress. There was something primitive about them, and a dignity of self-possession that the crabs lacked, swarming all over each other and scuttling into corners. One of the fishermen – Tony, the tall, clean-shaven one with the slow Somerset accent – was explaining to the Dawson children that one big claw was used for crushing its prey, and the other for cutting it up. The four smaller claws were like forks, lifting the food to the lobster's mouth. And lobsters could be left or right-handed, like people. He picked up a couple of big ones and held them out towards the little boys – 'Test it for yourselves!' until they retreated, squealing with delight, to their mother's long skirt. I couldn't blame them: putting out a hand towards a lobster triggered an instant response. Its black eyes would swivel on their stalks, and big pincer claw lift in a threatening gesture, even though it was made harmless by two thick elastic bands.

I walked back up the track with Nellie's daughter Jane and her baby, Kevin, who was soon to have his first birthday. Her other son was eight. It was because of him and the need to go to school that the family had made the decision to leave the island. 'We didn't go far, only to Aberdaron. But it's another world, really. I like to bring them back every summer. It's still my home really, where I lived all my life.'

I asked if she had been born here, and she shook her head. 'On the mainland, and so was my brother Ernest. My mother went home to her mam to have us, it was the way in those days The "old people" as we call them, who had lived on Bardsey for generations, they gave birth on the island – all their family was here – but nearly all of them left in the Twenties.' As I pushed the pram, she talked of the island-born she remembered. 'The last baby born on the island . . . I suppose it must have been my cousin in 1951 at Cristin, but it wasn't planned to happen here, the weather must have turned rough. That often happened, you can see from some of the names – there was Gwyndon, he was in school with me. His name means "white wave", and Gwynfor is "white sea". And there was one little boy actually born in the boat on the way over. The story goes that his dad had to be stopped from cutting the cord with his old bait knife, all rusty and fishy as they are . . .'

She glanced up at the school perched on a small apron of grass above the road. 'When I went to school, there were fifteen or sixteen of us there, a few children from most houses and more from some. There were eight from Rhedynogoch, next door to us!' She named them, ticking them off on her fingers. 'But that family left when I was seven. My father took over their land and the house stayed empty, it still is. When the school closed, that was it. Young people don't want to come here and work hard and then have to start again when their children are school age. And it's not a place to be old, the work's too hard. I'll be glad when my parents give up the farm and come to live on the mainland.'

She gave me a quick, assessing glance. Taller and slimmer than her mother, she resembled her in hair and bearing, and the strength of gaze. Then, as though she'd made her mind up: 'You'll be a help to Rilda,' she offered. 'We like that. She works hard, always having people to stay. She's been very good to us. Did you know she taught Ernest to swim? None of us had ever learned; very few fishermen can swim, it's almost a superstition with them not to. And some of the younger lighthouse-keepers as well, even though they laughed at her.

'Now, would you like a quick look inside the school?'

Behind the door, a row of wooden pegs at varying heights and a steel water tank with a lead tap at bucket height and a thick slate lid. On her brother Ernest's first day at

school, Jane told me, he'd run away because he was sure the teacher was trying to poison him by suggesting he drink from the tap – diesel and paraffin, he knew, came from tanks like that. 'But there were only seven or eight children in school, so she ran after him and brought him back. And I think he had a *chwip din* from my mother.' She'd finished her schooling by then, I supposed? 'Of course! I was about twenty by then . . .'

All the same, I thought she looked around the little schoolroom with fondness when we stepped inside, and tutted about the disarranged furniture – small chairs and tables piled higgledy-piggledy and cupboard doors hanging askew, dusty books spilling to the wooden floor. The air still held a memory of chalk, old paper and polish, and it was warm although the room was open to the pitched roof and the slates, with sturdy cross-beams where a brass lamp was hanging.

There used to be two, she said, and they could be raised or lowered by a thin chain. The Observatory had recently been given the use of the building as a ringing room, and they were going to clear it soon; she wondered what would happen to the piano and the pianola, one each side of the west-facing windows. The pianola had been a great novelty (a present to the school from somebody important, she seemed to remember, perhaps Mrs Lloyd George). It came with a box of paper rolls of different tunes, and when a roll was slotted in properly, the keys went up and down as if played by invisible hands. 'We all loved that, pretending to play, and one or two of us learned quite well.' She was going to show me how it worked but there was no sign of the rolls in the cupboards or behind the remains of the oak-panelled *sêt fawr* that leaned the length of the back wall.

There was a fireplace with a tall metal guard: 'In winter, we used to pretend we had a cold or a cough so we could sit near it, with the little ones.' Now it was screened by a dark oak bookcase with *Llyfrgell Ynys Enlli* in gold lettering across the top. I pulled out a book in dark blue covers, with Bardsey Council School March 1932 inscribed on the fly-leaf, and in a child's careful round handwriting, William Thomas Evans, Cristin. A collection of prayers and hymns, arranged for different age groups, it fell open at *Iesu, Cofia'r Plant* (Jesus, Remember the Children). It used to be a favourite, said Jane, and she read the first verse aloud, translating for me: *Draw, draw yn China a thiroedd Japan*: Far off, far off in China and the lands of Japan/ little yellow children live . . .

I was moved, partly perhaps by the sound and rhythm of the language, but by the idea of the handful of children in this green place earnestly singing about heat and famine and ignorance, feeling themselves part of a larger family and collecting pennies for the missionary cause ('for the black babies' as we used to call it in the little schools of the Fifties). 'We did a lot of geography,' said Jane. 'I've always been glad of that, to know where I am in the world.'

On the teacher's desk lay the dusty black Attendance Register 1948/9. I lingered on my own to flick through the lists of dates and names. *Reasons for Absence: Cold; Bronchitis; Illness of Mother; Sore Throat;* and then, as the farming year progressed, *Haymaking; Cow Calving; Shearing,* and, once, *Accompanying Father to Mainland.* The careful handwriting, each week's tidy totals and signature, bore witness to a way of life that had passed, with priorities we had all once shared. The only surprise, if I thought about it, was that the entirely Welsh-speaking, Welsh-thinking life of this community twenty years ago was recorded only in English.

Seal Cave

Ernest – pronounced with the stress on the second syllable, Ur-*nest* – was central to Rilda's talk of the island: what a skilful boatman he was, with an instinctive knowledge of the currents; how he'd worked at the lighthouse after leaving school, and was a natural mechanic, keeping the old tractors and the generator going. How he'd wanted to go to sea, to join the navy as an engineer but had been disappointed because of his short sight. 'Everybody' hoped he would settle into farming and take over when his father retired, because otherwise what would happen? Why didn't more young people want to come and make a living on the island?

On Tuesday we were still sitting at supper when there was a tap at the door, and he walked in. He was just out to see if he could get a few rabbits in Nant Withy, he said,

and his mother had asked him to call in to see if Sophie's cold was better. He leaned his shotgun against the door jamb and sat down for a *paned*. While Rilda made the tea, she got him talking about the lobster prices, and what the weather was likely to do (they had a generator down at Tŷ Pella and watched the BBC forecasts on television.) Shearing and haymaking – had they gone well? There were still a few ewes hiding on the back of the mountain, he said, looking, I thought, rather harassed at being interrogated.

'I've been telling Christine about Seal Cave –' Rilda began.

'Would you like to see it?' and at my surprised nod, 'Let's go now.'

Taken aback, I muttered something, to which, already on his feet, he replied airily, 'It won't take long. What have you got on your feet? – No walking boots, I suppose? Well, they'll do. I'll come back for that –' nodding towards the gun, and then he was out through the door. Rilda volunteered young David to come as well, and called after us, 'Take the torch!'

We set off up the path I knew but soon veered steeply round the north-east shoulder. The day was sinking into grey, the sky overcast but with soft, plumpy clouds, so we were not moving into shadow as we skirted the gull colony – quiet now as the birds were settling for sleep – and picked a way along a sheep-track no more than an instep wide through dry grass and rock. On the left, the ground tilted sheer to the endlessly shifting sea. Beyond it, the mainland was a wavering line of smudged charcoal. The islander moved ahead lightly, his tread as easy as if he were sauntering on a level pavement, and we trudged or teetered behind him. Eventually he halted, waiting for first David and then myself to catch up. He pointed: 'It's straight down there.' At the foot of the perilously steep slope – no bushes, or even bracken, to hang on to – there was a great tumble of grey rock that had slid down the hillside and on down into the depths. It looked very far away.

When Ernest squatted and sat down, I thought that was it – we'd rest a bit and then go back the way we'd come. But, bending his left leg under him, he leaned back on it and began to scoot down the slope on his behind. Then, using the right leg as a brake, he looked back at us. 'That's the easiest way – it's quite safe, come on.' It was amazingly reassuring to get lower (not so far to topple, sighed the brain, illogically, ignoring the hundred feet or so of fall). Once in direct contact with the ground, my body relaxed and I found myself enjoying the exhilaration and the silliness of sliding down the slippery grass to arrive in a laughing heap at the bottom.

Clambering among the tumble of boulders emphasised their giant scale and that of the forces that had wrenched them off the mountain. Where a particularly imposing flat slab lay tipped at an angle, Ernest stopped. 'There are two ways in,' he told us. 'You can edge round the base of this rock – there's a fair-sized hole into the cave but you have to hang from your fingertips and stretch to find the ledge inside with your feet. David's tall enough, but you'd better go in under here.'

It was a narrow triangular opening below the great slab, a jagged mouth into the dark.

'Lie on your back and slide in, feet first. We'll go round and catch you.'

Awkwardly I lowered myself and inserted my feet, grasping the overhang. I was going to do this. His voice came from below, muffled by layers of earth and stone: 'Right, now you.'

Lying back, I wriggled and slithered into a slimy tunnel. There was a flicker of ancient terror as my face passed under the rock. There is something appalling about slipping away from the sky with eyes open, going under and into the earth and sensing the weight above, the poise and delicate balance of it, but knowing that its timescale, the rhythm of its seasons, is so utterly beyond ours that we can only register it as a vast indifference. And having to let go with no purchase for the feet either – but then my left arm was grasped firmly and I was guided down. I felt his solidity and strength through the warmth of flesh, and then I was crouching on wet rock, peering about. There was the sound and smell of water, and as my eyes adjusted to the dimness I could make out its shifting skin below and a diffused gleam from an underwater entrance. Dark, clammy walls enclosed us. David was a blacker shape a few feet away. It felt like a stone hut, the sort of place where Inuit hunters might wait for their totem animal to emerge (yes, cold and remote) or Celtic hermits pray and fast until they conjured visions.

33

I don't know how long we sat without speaking in the sloosh and slap of the tide coming within walls, water's restlessness at being restrained. In a while there were the louder splashes and snorts of a seal surfacing, becoming aware of our presence on the ledge, and retreating indignantly, unseen. David switched the torch on and played its beams across the deep-shadowed angles and crevices. There was a hint of sadistic glee in the way he announced that he was looking for the spiders – special gigantic cave spiders, white and blind because they spend their whole lives in the dark. I looked, and saw webs but no spiders, and told him smugly I didn't mind spiders, anyway. The cobwebs strung from corner to corner were huge, though. The enclosure – not much bigger than a garden shed – was not a real cave hollowed and smoothed out by the sea but an accidental space created by the rockfall. The flattish slab on which we crouched tilted down into the water, its roughnesses glistening with salt. Lower rocks, partly submerged, made a kind of beach where the seals hauled out. The walls were shiny with moisture – and a flicker in the torchlight betrayed a pale spider clambering with enormously long legs towards a cluster of eggs hanging from the roof like unripe fruit.

We came out into the quiet evening, the air welcoming and warm, and watched the displaced seal bobbing safely offshore, watching us. The sea was slowly turning to ink, spreading out from the shadow of the island, but the sky over the mountain was bright. A stony little trail just above the rocks, the bottom path of three, led south in a gentle curve, and for a little while we followed it in single file. Then Ernest said, 'This is taking too long. Let's go straight up –' and as an afterthought, 'You all right?'

It was less precipitous here, but still so steep I found myself almost on hands and knees, pulling myself up. Soon it became obvious that my sensible shoes would not 'do', so I carried them and slipped and clambered barefoot. Straight up we went, avoiding the bracken and the boulder scree called Briw Gerrig, the Hurt of Stones, where Ernest pointed to another cave higher up, 'Big enough to stand up in, and it goes quite deep into the mountain, with a chimney climb. Tricky even in daylight.'

Reaching a shallow cwm near the top, he held out a hand to help me over the rocky crest, and as I grasped it I felt the smallness of my bones within palms broadened by heavy work and hauling ropes; there were pads of callus at the base of the fingers. We sank into the springy heather triumphant, sweat cooling on our faces, and sprawled looking out over the fields that were still lit by the western sky, and towards unseen horizons over the rim of the turning world. The lighthouse's steady wink was almost mesmerizing. We sat until Ernest realized he'd better get home for the forecast, so if we were sure of the way back he'd go down over Pen Cristin; he'd call for his gun another time. He stood for a moment though, with head tilted as if listening; then 'There's a swell building by the rocks. I wouldn't be surprised if there's a change in the weather tomorrow.' And he was gone, nimble among the shadows until he merged with them.

We walked slowly back along the ridge. Lights were prickling into view, tiny constellations against the dark, all the way down the curve of Cardigan Bay. David picked out Harlech, Barmouth, Aberystwyth. 'Sometimes you can see Pembrokeshire,' he said.

As we came over the hill in the slow, sweet dusk, Venus was rising bright in the west. A little owl called from the tangle of wild hops and elderberries behind Nant, and oil lamps glowed orange in kitchen and bedroom.

Lighthouse

For two days the fog came back, woolly damp and smothering as if a shorn fleece had been thrown over us. The foghorn lowed, on and on, over and over. When the fog was thickest, it sounded sad and distant, like a cow that's calling a lost calf without much hope. As the pale disc of the sun tried to break through, it combed the mist into glistening strands, and then the foghorn was much louder, blasting its warning of danger, bellowing harshly five times a minute. The grass was slippery, everywhere strange. But when I waded through the wet vegetation following the mountain path, I broke through into brilliant sunshine and strode along the ridge in an exaltation of brightness, walking a causeway above the clouds.

We cut the grass in next door's garden, or rather David did, with a *cryman* borrowed from the farm – a small arc of razor-sharp steel, its curved ash handle worn smooth by many hands. I was familiar with its English name, sickle, only from reading Hardy's novels. I stood by with my wooden hay-rake feeling like Tess on a quiet day. The muscles in my legs were still stiff from the climb.

One afternoon I baked my first loaf of bread to Rilda's precise requirements. 'Lukewarm, I said! That'll kill the yeast – dip your finger in to test it.' It came out of the oven more like a brick than anything I'd ever eaten but she said it was a start. A Victoria sponge was more successful (I remembered to use a wooden spoon, *and* to dust the tin with flour), but apparently it came out of the oven light, fragrant and golden because of the fresh farm eggs. 'You can't go wrong with eggs like that.'

On another we helped to get the sheep in – I was despatched to stand in a gap and wave my arms if any came my way. Going down through the misty fields was like wading through quicksilver, everything shimmering in a diffused radiance: the cloud was thinning, the foghorn losing confidence in itself, becoming tinny. It was very still in my patch. I waited, in a timeless circle of cheeping calls from meadow pipits. Briefly, the sun broke through and laid a warm hand across my shoulders, and all around the grass and leaves seemed to exhale and lie back to bask.

But the sheep were running. There were bleats getting closer and rustlings in the thickets of bulrush and bracken. I stood to attention as first a posse and then a stream of ewes trundled by, followed by the dogs, tongues lolling, and young Iain, Wil's eight-year-old grandson, running with them. He sent me a grin that lit up his whole face, and dashed on into the fog. Then Wil himself, steady, in his salt-stained denim jacket and cap, using his stick to direct Pegi, his old brown sheepdog who was deaf. I could hear shouting and a motorbike, but the drive had passed me by. Lethargically, I followed an old path which turned out to lead up and round to the back of Tŷ Nesa, where Tony had his makeshift wind-generator, not stirring at all in the calm air.

Almost every day I had to 'pop down' for vegetables from Mary's garden. Though built to the same plan as Rilda's, her house had a completely different outlook and atmosphere. While Nant was enclosed by buildings and dominated by the ruined tower and its Celtic crosses, Tŷ Nesa looked out on two sides to the sea and at the back on to a walled garden full of ripening green and colour. I had picked the last of the year's blackcurrants here, while the children popped flowers off the fuchsias, big cerise and magenta danglers that they hung about their ears. There were neat rows of cabbages and crisp-headed lettuces, the dark curls of kale and miniature trees of sprouting broccoli. Between carefully-staked rows of peas and beans, interspersed with sweet peas, the feathery foliage of carrots provided a contrast for the eye. 'You can grow anything here if you can only give it shelter from the wind,' Mary used to say, and went some way to proving it.

I hardly remember the evenings, except for the Seal Cave one. I took Chaddie the black spaniel for evening walks along the road and looked longingly for the Irish hills at sunset. Perhaps I sat and read under the gas lamp while Rilda sewed curtains for next door and Sophie fiddled with a sun-hat, David with cards spread across the coffee table for one of his interminable games of patience. And I wrote my journal, of course, every night except the first. Scribbling in a blue school exercise book, in a candlelit daze, I re-lived the sights and sounds and voices of the day, sitting up in bed, waiting for shearwaters.

On Thursday, Ernest called to collect his gun. 'Rilda says you'd like to see the lighthouse. I'm going down tomorrow . . . And the fog's supposed to clear by morning.'

I walked beside him the length of the stony beach called Henllwyn. The tide was out, leaving an apron of seaweed, kelp draped across the rocks like khaki uniforms laid out to dry, each stem the length of a man, with fronds like fingers. The thick clump of root I learned was called a 'holdfast'. I liked the name, but the pungency was a bit too much. Heavy on the iodine, maybe.

The approach to the lighthouse felt strangely formal. We walked along a dead straight, smooth road gravelled underfoot, with the remains of white pillars and gates barring the way and the Trinity House flag flying from the miniature castle of its flagstaff enclosure. Inside the white gate was another world; the near military order and neatness was striking. Sunshine bounced off white walls, lending the enclosure a Mediterranean brilliance. The grass had a nap like velvet; the gravel was raked, the separate garden

37

plots weed-free and colourful, with some flowers bright among the usual vegetables. Each keeper had his own plot, so there was a spirit of competition. They also had, as my companion pointed out on the walk back, plenty of time, for one day in every three was officially leisure, to make up for an all-night shift, the 'middle watch' from midnight till eight in the morning.

I recognised a ritual in the way we were greeted and invited into the keepers' bungalow for a cup of tea. It was a relief to put some walls between my ears and the noise of heavy diesel engines pounding away, though I soon stopped noticing it. The living room where we sat was stuffy: the heating was kept on summer and winter, and one or more of the easy chairs occupied day and night. John Bell made tea (with a choice of a spoonful of condensed milk or a shake of the powdered stuff) while Pat Murphy talked, half an eye on the TV in the corner. He was officially on watch. So no important message would be missed, the big radio-telephone was turned to full volume and from time to time it sputtered into insistent life, so loud that I could hardly understand the blurred words, let alone the codes. There was an exchange of numbers with someone called Charlie George, but it was a source of great amusement that I had not realised this was radio-speak for 'Coastguard.'

The tower was almost a hundred feet high to the lantern. It was square, and built of big limestone blocks, not plastered or lined on the inside so that it enclosed a chill, echoing space that smelled like a garage workshop. It was hollow, empty except for the stairwell of stone steps with metal handrails. There were three landings, and windows on different sides, so as I climbed in a slow spiral I could catch glimpses of the ground falling away – the other buildings getting smaller, grass and rocks to the south, then sea and sky until the final steep iron ladder to the metal floor of the lantern platform with its giant lens floating on its bath of mercury encased in steel. It had a glasshouse heat and when Pat pushed aside heavy curtains, its glare too, but the smells were not of growing but of hot oil, hot metal.

The lantern was a huge glass eye, the lightbulb (only 400 watts) encased in an intricate nest of glass, those five etched and serrated lenses that gave the flashes and threw them twenty miles through the dark. Diamond-like facets glinted and shivered, even though the lantern wasn't moving. The curtains had to be drawn as soon as the light was stopped, at sunrise and sunset, or the prisms would work in reverse, concentrating and focusing the sun as a burning glass until the whole thing went up in flames. 'It's the main reason for us being here,' Pat said. 'If they could find a way of doing that with light sensors, we'd be out of a job. All the other things can be made automatic.'

He bent down to usher me through a small door that gave on to a narrow walkway outside. Brightness, exposure after enclosure, the tilting sensation of a high narrow perch in empty air, made me catch my breath and cling momentarily to the gallery rails.

Looking at the island from this height put it all back together again, as I had seen it on that first afternoon – a small world, in balance with the vast reaches of sea and sky. Faint drifts of mist still moved across so that layers of soft-focus alternated with areas of clear vision – and, yes, it was almost like a vision or a mirage of landfall, a long curve of land swelling to the mountain, sloping to the shoulder that protected the bay, and petering out into the narrow neck of green to the fringe of black rocks and gullies beyond the lighthouse. A slight breeze trembled the thin scarves of fog, and then the view solidified into a homely, known place. The houses dotted along the track seemed planted, to be growing out of the place rather than imposed upon it (they were not painted white as they are now.) Where land met the sea its edge was highlighted in silver, sometimes intensified by a wave breaking into white spray, but all mute, like a film without a sound track.

'It'd be hard to live here without the lighthouse,' Ernest remarked on our way back across the Narrows. 'I sometimes think that's why Bardsey still has people farming it, really living on it, when most of the Welsh islands – Skomer, Skokholm, Ramsey – are just bird islands now. They've been talking for years about making all the Lights automatic. If that happens, that place will be dead. It'll be a sad day for Bardsey when there are no more keepers here.'

I got back to bad news and long faces at Nant. Rilda was lying on the sofa with a wet tea-towel wrapped round her leg. Tidying a high shelf, she had slipped from the

stool and landed awkwardly, wrenching her ankle painfully. 'That's all it is, I'm sure it's not broken. But such a nuisance!' She was cross with herself, and wretched about the church group; it was too late to cancel, but how could she cope? Sophie sat close, literally wringing her hands, making tentative offers of support from time to time: 'I can peel potatoes if someone brings them to me,' and 'If I had a high stool I could wash dishes.' Eva, it transpired – who could have helped – was away again the following week. I felt helpless as Sophie as I wondered aloud what use I might be, if I could arrange to stay . . . and saw Rilda's expression change as she worked out a strategy. 'Well – I suppose I could give you instructions . . . it wouldn't be easy – but at least you don't have ideas of your own about cooking. You haven't picked up many *bad* habits.'

She was a teacher with a project. 'We'll make a start by writing down my recipes for the basics. Where's that notebook of yours?'

So it was that my stay on the island was extended. And by the end of that second week, with Rilda on her feet again, I didn't want to leave. I went home for a change of clothes, came back to stay with the Atkinsons at Tŷ Nesa, and felt myself growing into the life of the island.

And the consequence was . . .

It was the dark of the moon that week. Each night after supper we walked and talked; not by formal arrangement, but whichever path I chose, his seemed to converge before too long. We sat in the heather or looking out at the sea as night thickened round us and the lighthouse flashes strengthened. And I experienced for the first time what it's like to stand in the dark and watch the wing of light sweeping towards you. Wait for it, then a blinding instant full face before it's travelling away again over the dark sea, succeeded by four swift surges, not so intense. With your back to the lighthouse you see its beams, like spokes of a great wheel of illumination, chase each other over the mountain – one long slow stroke; another; pause, then a quick sneaky one, followed by a shy glance, and a final full flash. Blackness while you count, and then it begins again.

If you keep your gaze on one object – the white rock on the mountain, for instance, or the marble gravestone of Lizzie from the lighthouse – as the beams come round, with each flash it comes sharply into focus, a pulse of light that lends a sense of presence, as if the stone had a heart-beat or was taking slow breaths.

We learned each other's features by that wheeling light, the wheeling stars, the shearwaters' arcing calls as they tried to earth themselves or went round again, screaming. One night the sky was ablaze with the cold fire of shooting stars, hundreds of them skimming overhead, brilliant against the delicate gauze of the Milky Way. The rock I leaned against gave off the day's warmth like a cooling chimney, the sea sighed and shifted, seals on Carreg Rhona howled a weave of voices distant and unreadable as the swirls of Ogam script on the ancient stones in the ruined Abbey.

Easing myself quietly into the sleeping house, fumbling my way into bed, I felt insubstantial as a shadow compared with all that still going on out there, the real world I'd been part of for a few hours, vivid, fully alive.

That same sense of unreality, of contrast that challenged my whole idea of self, asserted itself suddenly one afternoon halfway through the Christmas term when I was back in the classroom, tidy and correct, teaching *Lycidas* to my A Level English group. In Milton's elegy for his friend drowned crossing the Irish Sea in 1637, the poet – working with a map, presumably – imagines the body drifting north along the north-west coast of Wales, naming Anglesey and the estuary of the Dee at Chester. But the two lines before that came swimming into sharp focus:

> Where were ye, Nymphs, when the remorseless deep
> Closed o'er the head of your lov'd Lycidas?
> For neither were ye playing on the steep
> Where your old Bards, the famous Druids, lie,
> Nor on the shaggy top of Mona high,
> Nor yet where Deva spreads her wisard stream.

'The steep' had to be Bardsey.

At once the island, never far from my thoughts these days anyway, sprang into my mind.

I was hooked. After forty years, I am still hooked. Since that first week, the island has become either 'here' (when I am on it) or 'there', when I am away from it. I have landed and walked up the stony track many times, not always with delight but invariably with a sense of coming home. There have been other expeditions to Ogo' Morlo, the seal cave, creeping in without disturbing the snorer below, or sitting still enough to watch sunlight dance and untwist itself into different colours underwater until the seals have come back in and flopped on to the rocks, fishy-breathed. I have polished the brass rails in the lighthouse and mopped down its one hundred and thirteen steps more times than I can count, while Ernest and our son service the machinery that keeps the light turning. Each August the earth has swung through the tail of the comet Swift-Tuttle and I have looked for meteor showers, knowing they are there but like so much of what goes on in the natural world, invisible. I have searched but failed to find the missing Attendance Register, but week by week from May until October I walk up to the school, lift the latch and push open the old door to welcome visitors and share with them stories of the island.

Awake at night on the mainland I imagine it as a parent wonders about her child. *The tamarisk tree outside Tŷ Pella must be sighing and bending in this westerly wind; how far will the lighthouse beams show through this fog, will our windows be blank tonight? How high are the waves running up the beach under the full moon?* Sometimes I wake with a dreamed image of some detail fading: close-up of a patch of silver hair-grass on the bank near the school, or of gazing into Ffynnon Corn, the monks' well. The stiff gold of a carline thistle prickles under my hand on Pen Cristin; rock braces me, wrapped in cold wind; stonechats chatter. I come out of darkness over a ridge and feel my face opening to light and warmth.

It is the great fact of my life, the place that chose me and where I became the person I am, or the better part of it.

from Signals

Once, from wherever on the island
I set out, our paths would close.
As at a time agreed for meeting
our random walks must touch

and flow together in a shining curve
as though there was a flavour
or a throb of earth at evening
our bodies learned to follow . . .

And in some ways still the same
as when we first slid home at night together
in the long cool stroke
the lighthouse smooths on sea and pasture.

Forty summers further on
you, attuned to every stone or
track-twist, still have to tell me
'Wait till the beam comes round'

and I forget to look out for my feet
gazing up at an inverted ocean
where shearwaters' white bellies swim
between pricked bubbles that are stars

night opening before us at each step
the great sky whirling and calling,
stumbling back after midnight beside you
as I choose still to do.

44

49

58

living on the island

Passing On

Driftwood crackles and spits in the small iron grate. Though it is only late August the fire is a comfort and point of focus, a distraction from the gale blustering up from the south-west, from the grey window with its view of white-lipped sea. An afternoon at the tail-end of a week of relentless wind and rain. We have just had tea; I can still taste Nellie's *cacan mwyar duon,* that delicious combination of crisp pastry and soft, sweet blackberries. I call her 'Nain' now, Granny. Her third grandchild, my son, (*another bloomin' boy!*) is helping with the washing up, sitting on the table next to the plastic bowl of soapy water. She scrubs each cup and saucer and plate, rubbing teaspoons to a shine. While Colin names and counts them, she keeps up a constant murmur of loving encouragement: '*Ie, 'ngwas i*', '*Da iawn, hogyn clyfar*', '*Hen gena bach!*'

Opposite me in the high-backed chair, Wil sighs and stretches long legs towards the grate, easing his bad knee. His hand is brown, scarred, thick-skinned. He pulls his baccy pouch from a pocket, looks at it wistfully, and with a glance at the weather, puts it down carefully beside the lamp. He sighs. I feel his glance on me, so I look up from last week's *Cambrian News*. His eyes are very blue; they are keen, like a sheepdog with too much energy. He's been cooped up here for a week, in the one-room school where he and Nellie spend the summers since they gave up the farm. He needs something to do, something to chase.

'How long now since you came to Enlli the first time?' he asks, in English. My Welsh is good enough to understand that Nellie is calling Colin a clever boy and a little rascal, but not up to a proper conversation. I calculate backwards for a second, and tell him, ten years.

'And who was here then? The warden at Cristin must have been George. Had Tony and Mary left? And what about all the other houses?'

We go through them, and he starts to talk about older times and tenants. At some point I find out the notebook I always have stuffed into a pocket and start scribbling names and dates, though most of the anecdotes take too much time to transcribe. Stories and details are still bubbling up as I bundle Colin into his all-in-one waterproof for the walk back to Rhedynogoch, where we now live for the fishing season every year, and so I ask whether he would mind having his memories recorded. His face lights up with enthusiasm. Behind us, I hear a quiet sound that could be a snort of derision. 'He'll like *that*,' Nellie says, not unkindly. She might not have heard of feminism, but she has clear ideas about the importance of women in this sort of life.

So through that autumn and winter, people and events of the island's last fifty years spring to life in my imagination and in Wil's words, on long spools of brown magnetic tape whirring slowly round. First on the island in the school and then on the mainland, once the clocks go back, my three-year-old plays with Lego on the hearth-rug or helps Nain wind wool into skeins while we talk history. Wil and I pore over copies of census records gleaned from the archives in Caernarfon and share the excitement when, deciphering the names of a family in 1851 I read out 'Henry, aged 3 months' and Wil exclaims 'Harri Cristin!' He tells me how he used to sneak out of school every chance he got to hang around the smithy in Aberdaron, the hub of the village then. 'There was always something going on, you got all the news there. And it was warm in winter.' The Bardsey boys often came in – big, swaggering men they were, especially the brothers from Cristin, strong enough to pick up the anvil and carry it to the boat for a dare. And one day – it must have been when he was older, because he had started work by then – he'd been sent down with a mare that had cast a shoe ploughing, and while he was standing holding her head, the men came in and told how Harri died. He'd been out round the pots early, then working in the fields all day, and when he came in he slumped on to the bench by the table and said he didn't want any *lobscows*. Mari, his sister, wasn't very pleased, but she went and boiled an egg. He ate it slowly. Then he put down the spoon, laid both arms on the table and his head went down among the dishes, and – pfff, he was dead. It took three of the island's strongest to lift him.

'A clever man, he was, Harri Williams. He was a great reader and he could remember everything he read. Whenever he came to Aberdaron he'd always buy a Welsh newspaper and take it round to read to the old ones on the island. He always had a joke and a word for us boys. Yes – he ate a boiled egg, and died.'

Wil feels a bond with the *hen bobl*, the old island people; his grandmother was born over there, or her mother, anyway, and he grew up with the stories and old names of places. I'm not sure whether he knew the island before his father John took the tenancy of Cristin in 1926, but he always had the shape of the community in his head. They were a special people, like one family, he tells me; they had disagreements, and learned to live with them. They just got on with life, put up with each other, and shared everything in times of need. After they left the island in a body they found it hard to live in separate places: they missed the casual, daily contact and knowledge of what was going on in their own small world. A number of them died quite soon, he says; in a few months, or years. But they were old, of course. That's why they left, mostly. 'A place for young people, this is. Strong young ones who come with little do well. Those who come here with money and think they can make it easy, they go without anything.'

Some of the islanders' names he recites testify to houses crumbled back into earth or plundered for farm buildings. He remembers Bridget Penyfron, who grew up in a crogloft cottage like Carreg Bach on the bank between the school and Tŷ Pella. 'When she was old she lived in Aberdaron. She talked about the island in the old days, the people behind us, and then she'd give me a *tamaid*, a little cake, for the walk home.'

Sure enough, I find a house called Penyfron in the census, and there is Bridget, and later I read accounts of children playing in the ruins in the second decade of the twentieth century. Wil's life is people and the land, his own world. He has a vivid curiosity about anyone who comes into it, taking it almost as a right to question visitors

Hands

Look at eighty years in these hands:
still strong, work-broadened, but listless, shiny
with swelling over the knuckles now.

Years she has spent
thinking through her hands.

Buried to the palms
in warm flour or earth or water
flowing through the spread web of her fingers;
briskly kneading dough to rise
or the flaccid newborn calf to breathe;
coaxing milk from a ripe udder; gathering stooks,
     picking berries;
scrubbing rinsing wringing smoothing folding;
sliding through the blind tight tunnel
to reach the lamb with one leg back;
slapping butter into shape. Testing
if the cake is cooked, if the child has fever

her hands came strong and clever, wide awake.

I could sew anything, you know. And knit. And
    mending –
every night, by lamplight. Never a chance to be still.

Once in summer, her fingers palely
crawling through soil all afternoon
purposeful as roots, then slid down fetlock stems
to hunt the weeds by feel, bare arms paddling in
    the dark
green swell of the potato ridges,
she felt the sun ripening so quickly out of mist
it seemed as if it could at any moment
split its skin and ooze
juice – a red volcanic flow, to scald her back.
She paused, looked up, and the world grew steady.

Held in her lap, her hands
clutch one another, keeping themselves still,
while the machine records
her husband's reminiscences.

about their origins and occupations. He has never got much from television. The wireless is good for weather and the news, but what matters to him is his own square mile, as he calls it. And you need to walk to know it; even on the mainland in winter, he refuses a lift in the Land-Rover to the village. 'You don't see anything from a car. You don't talk to anybody or see what's growing. You don't smell the air.'

Is it a known phenomenon that, nearing the end of life, there is an urge to tell stories, to pass on something of what's been learned? I have come across it more than once not always from the elderly; or perhaps it is only with hindsight that conversations take on a special significance when there is no chance of continuing them. There are so many questions I would have asked Wil, so many pages and even sentences left for another day. The following spring he too was gone, collapsing almost as suddenly as Harri Cristin.

This is where my hunger for the island's social history starts, and frustration because there are no books that lay it all out neatly solved. I must actively search out people with memories of living there and try and cross-check them, peering to make out erratic handwriting on census forms until evolving surnames dance before my eyes like a flick-book: ap Richard, Pritchard, splitting into Rhisiart, Richards, before they are replaced by Joneses and Griffithses. I spend hours closed in with paper or scanning microfiches in the archives at Caernarfon and the National Library. On good days it was an excavation, working backwards through the layers. Not so much research as a sporadic, undisciplined fossicking on the borderland between social history and myth, and all fired by a moment of enthusiasm shared thirty years ago.

Nellie had her stories too but I recorded them only in my memory, so they have become part of my sense of that world.

Scatterings

Perhaps even the hunter-gatherers were not the first. Before it was an island, this hump of land must have beckoned across mosquitoed marshland and river swollen still with meltwater. For hundreds of generations, people have been drawn here: they have left

evidence going back perhaps nine thousand years to the Mesolithic period of the Stone Age in scatterings of stone chipped and sharpened into tools. The first worked flints were picked up from crumbling hedge boundaries in Carreg fields, then along the north-west, and latterly in Tŷ Pella potato patch. Once archaeologists started really looking, thousands of flakes, blades and cores were recovered from ploughed land and earth banks undermined by shearwaters. One site especially drew their interest: where the stream runs down to Bae Rhigol, so many worked flint tools and waste material implied a settlement or at least a regular working area, although nobody has yet found a hearth. Without ash or the remains of living material, there is no way of knowing how long ago or how long our ancestors were here.

The stone itself would have been carried here by ice, or the sea, or the stoneworkers themselves: a lump the size of a fist could provide many blades and scrapers for this hunter-gatherer clan following herds of reindeer, elk, wild horses. These were people literally in step with their world and the cycles of nature: they had seasonal camps, places they returned to as the animals followed the grazing, or where the elders knew there was food to be harvested. Perhaps they came to the western shore and the hill that was Bardsey in the hungry time of early spring, to pick limpets off the rocks and gather winkles and whelks when the tide retreated, the 'famine food' that may explain why our species hugged the coastline as it spread north out of Africa.

I imagine them, a small group of eight or twelve, sharing food and company by the fire before moving on. There's a granny sheltering a sick child, a couple of women with babies in fur slings, a thin girl pounding seeds on a flat rock while boys scamper and practise with their slingshots. A man squats, still chipping and shaping a blade or two, and around him the flakes of old working fallen abandoned, with the old tools that have lost their edge discarded. There's the thump and chip of hammer on stone all day long in this camp which looks back over the reedy saltmarsh to the dense scrub of the hills they have left. They know that when the moon gets full the horse-herds will sweep past. And here they have feasted, for the sea-birds have returned, and there's promise of eggs roasted in the embers. As they walk the shore, heads down, searching for the good stone, the women gather small shellfish and greenstuff – samphire, sea-kale, seaweed – to fill willow baskets slung on their backs. Back at the camp, the men are very particular, fumbling the stones, tossing them in the hand to gauge the density of each, judging how to find and coax sharp edges from its smoothness. There will be careful trimming of the chosen ones, shaping them into nodules, feeling for the split, the long parallel in the pattern of the rock; and then, the strike. From among the discards the women rummage for those from which fire springs when struck, kernels of sparks to be cradled in dried moss and wood-shavings when a flame needs kindling.

Among the scatters of worked stone are pebbles of creamy white chert and its darker, rich brown form alongside pale grey flint, almost translucent flakes, small sharp triangles, for arrowheads maybe or barbs on fishing spears – what the archaeologists call microliths, small flints that are part of a composite tool. There are also used blades and scrapers that may have been dropped and lost, or discarded because they'd lost their edge. Perhaps some of the accumulated flints were a cache of tools, hidden or stored for when they came this way again. Or an offering to the spirit of the place.

There's an ebb and flow of people everywhere but in places like this the marks of their passage last longer. The hunter-gatherer society was a successful, sophisticated one; it survived for far longer than ours has, and was far more sustainable. Nomads don't see landscape as something to be owned or controlled, rather they feel that they belong to it, and stories of particular paths and special places renew that kinship. Here was a place the flint-knappers came back to, each year or generation adding to a sense of attachment, stories waking in the minds of the old ones. There might have been ritual celebrations on the return to significant landmarks: surely the leaning block of limestone above Pen Cristin, catching the light at sunrise and reflecting the glow of sunset, must have been one such? From the sea it is a crooked finger, like Maen Melyn Llŷn, the standing stone on the headland opposite Bardsey; from the land below it seems to stretch wings like a big stone bird. And yet to us now it is all but nameless, just 'Carreg Wen', the White Rock.

The weather got warmer, the animals' migration routes shifted; perhaps some were managed so that human wandering became centred. In one place, they might have

found cached grain sprouting, and invented the idea of planting crops. Where there was fresh water, shelter, an unfailing stock of food from the sea and a defensible site, they settled. Crossing to Bardsey meant a sea-journey – but that would not have deterred our ancestors, resourceful navigators and boat-builders who rode the tides of air and water. There is a shell midden near Solfach from the times of the earliest farmers, mostly of limpets, winter or famine food. In 2007 part of a fine flint scraper was picked out of the soil there, worn smooth with use, fitting snugly in the palm with a groove for the thumb. It is probably Neolithic. And from pockets of cremated human remains uncovered by the sea on Henllwyn beach and from what are listed as Bronze Age cairns, we surmise that there were either people living here five millennia ago, or perhaps crossing the Sound in tiny skin boats to inter their dead: outlined as the island is against sunset, it has probably always seemed, from the mainland, a sort of threshold. When the fires were lit, or the ashes carefully buried, they would have been on cliffs or at the highest point of the mountain, looking out.

Bardsey was at the heart of trade routes for thousands of years. 'Called by Ptolemy *Edri* and by Pliny *Andros*, by us *Enlli*, it must have been a place of note as early as Roman times for Pliny, who died in AD79, to notice it,' wrote the scholar Richard Fenton in 1804. Ptolemy, in first-century Alexandria, drew the first map of the Irish Sea and Llŷn, probably getting his information from Phoenician traders, like those whose ship was wrecked in Porth Felen on the mainland coast, just opposite the island which might be identified as *Edri*. By then, the first of the huts, (*cytiau Gwyddelod*, as they are called in Welsh, Irishmen's huts) would have been occupied. Their builders chose a sheltered, dry spot. Perched high on a gently sloping plateau beneath the rocky ridge of the mountain, all the entrances face south, protected from the worst of the north and east winds. The sea they looked out over may have been much the same, as empty as ours, but the island was probably covered in low trees – willow, brambles, perhaps scrub oak. They had small, bendy wood, then, as well as stone, earth, and turf to make dwellings. If this was the end of a journey, the oxhide or deerskin hull of the boat could provide a weatherproof roof.

All that remains is a pattern of earth walls about the height of a small child. There are two groups of huts, a scattering of small round ones above the farm and some higher ones above Cristin that are easier to distinguish in the bracken, and suggestive of more organised living. Many more may have vanished, undermined by weather, rabbits and shearwaters and swamped by wild growth. The earliest Christian monks liked to live in tiny individual cells with a larger building for eating and possibly another for communal prayer, and there is a rectangular building here, the length of a large room – about the size of the school, in fact – with what seems to be a small field-system behind it; another two smaller round huts nearby are enclosed within a boundary wall. Perhaps this is the earliest Christian settlement on the island, the circular walls around a tiny chapel that gave the name 'llan' to so many places in Wales.

Nearby on the mainland there was a community of *multitudinem fratrum*, 'many brothers', as a fifth-century gravestone attests, and before them there would have been first missionaries from Gaul and Ireland, and probably a few seeking places to live apart from the world. These *peregrini* (wanderers) set out in small boats 'for the glory of God', as if pitting the force of the sea and their survival against the strength of their faith. They offered themselves up, sometimes not even steering, so that if they made landfall, it was with the confidence of knowing that that was where God wanted them to be.

The Exclusive Business of the Place

According to Edmund Hyde Hall in his *Description of Caernarvonshire* early in the nineteenth century, 'religion was, we are told, the exclusive business of the place', and for a thousand years, it certainly was.

By the year 500 it was already known as *ynys sanctaidd*, island of saints, and as a sanctuary, *insula sanctorum*. Soon after, Einion Frenin, the 'golden-handed Prince of Lleyn' who had already founded a monastery at Penmon on Anglesey with his brother Seiriol in charge, invited Breton monk Cadfan to undertake the same on Bardsey. Some time early in the sixth century (possibly 516), he arrived with twenty-five kinsmen, many of whose names have become part of the Welsh landscape. The island itself

seems to have been called 'Bangor Gadfan' at this time, suggesting a monastic teaching college, a sort of missionary school, named for its *penrhaith*, its lord, or chief.

There are no places on the island named for Cadfan, but a couple of fields commemorate his successor, Lleuddad (or Laudatus). I found Gerddi Lleuddad (Lleuddad's Gardens) marked on a 1790 map as 'gardens and tenement'. In spite of all the disruption caused by rebuilding, plants of medicinal value still grew in the rough pasture opposite the chapel door until a tree-planting scheme about fifteen years ago replaced them with fuchsia. Fortunately, a couple of thrifty islanders had already set cuttings in their gardens, so dark blue (and extremely poisonous) monkshood persists and elecampane sends up its big gold flowers each July as reminders of the time when its roots sliced in honey were a remedy for chest infections. Its power was such that it was called 'elfwort', magic plant, and according to the Physicians of Myddfai, it 'stays even the plague itself, God willing'.

There's nothing in the earliest stories about Lleuddad as gardener, but plenty about magic. We first hear of him as a member of a religious community on the mainland, but incurring displeasure because of his frequent disappearances; his brother monks insisted that he carry a bell at all times so they could follow his movements. When it was discovered that he travelled miraculously across the sea to Bardsey to commune more closely with God, it was put to Cadfan to persuade him to remain there, and on his deathbed, the first Abbot instructed the community to accept Lleuddad as their new leader. The other bishops – eleven of them – weren't willing to let a relative newcomer take over without a demonstration of power. Taking their staffs, Lleuddad stuck them in the earth, where they grew into a tree, which spread, and branched, and – as they watched – burst into leaf. 'Let him who will take his staff,' but none was able to until Lleuddad made the sign of the cross and the solid trunk split again. As a further miracle, he poured a bowl of milk into the well at the top of the field (or some say, milked a cow into it) and challenged the others to get it out without removing any water. Once he had succeeded, no one felt like challenging him any more.

It was Gwen Robson, summering in Plas Bach, who told me this story. I remembered evenings when the supper table had been cleared quickly before she arrived to spread the big map across it. When she came in, the room was suddenly warmer, brighter; there would be a short exchange in careful Welsh (it was a grief to her that she had been forced to learn as an adult, discouraged in childhood from picking up 'servants' language') and then we'd leave them to it, her eager questions about field names and Wil's painstaking answers.

'Fascinating!' we'd hear from the next room. Years later she walked me through the fields, talking fast and persuasively: 'Now, thanks to Wil, this is still called Cae Bryn Baglau, field of the hill of the staffs, and the well – small and overgrown as it is, almost forgotten! – must be Ffynnon y Dalar, the famous healing well! Isn't it amazing that the name has survived, through all the changes – from the Celtic cell, the Viking raids, the important Abbey, its destruction,' – she waved her arms as if simulating axe-blows – 'then the take-over by buccaneers and wild men, right down to the last members of the last living Welsh community here.' She paused for breath. 'Neither Wil nor I had any idea. Then I found it recorded both in Latin and medieval Welsh. The name was still in common use, though its origins were totally forgotten.'

Lleuddad's story goes on: when on his death-bed an angel appeared summoning him to heaven and saying 'Take whoever of thy monks thou choosest with thee,' his canons cried, 'We will all go!' The dying man (with a weary sigh, perhaps, a roll of the eyes, suggested Gwen) explained that the work of the monastery was too important for that. He persuaded the Angel of Death to concede that from that time on the monks should die from eldest to eldest in order of age, and that the soul of any person buried on the island should not go to hell, 'nor should any die by the way they should not be damned'. I never fully grasped the significance of this until I saw, in Italian churches, horribly graphic paintings of damnation: the medieval imagination would have seized any opportunity to insure against such torments. This tradition – and the celebrity saints buried there – made the island famous in the Wales of the Middle Ages, bringing processions of the faithful and monks carrying embalmed corpses from church to church along the pilgrim routes of Llŷn, as well as 'coffin ships' sailing out of Barmouth, Abererch and Caernarfon. The boast of 20,000 'saints, martyrs and confessors', generally

thought to owe something to poetic licence, begins to seem not so far-fetched: 'saint' simply signified a person of devout faith.

But of all these, only two fragments of what might be ancient gravestones – or cross-shafts – remain, and they can be seen in the chapel now. As the track becomes worn away by water, stone 'long cist' graves come to the surface, and have to be covered with soil or gravel. All this area was burial ground. Anyone who has lived on the island will have found human bones, I should think, especially at the North End; I saw skulls piled at the side of a trench dug for a generator exhaust in the Seventies. They were yellowed and very old, strong-jawed, with extremely ground-down teeth. It seemed more appropriate to bury them, with respect, nearby, than to send them off for dating and perpetual storage in a university department.

It is no wonder the monks survived to a good age, for they would have lived well, better than most in those times: meat three times a week, supplemented by fish, cheese and eggs on other days, washed down with ale. Bread would be baked on the island, oats and vegetables grown, and in 1291 there were 24 cattle, 120 breeding ewes and rabbits a-plenty: the Abbey made 35 shillings per annum from the sale of 'flesh and skins' of these alone. The original monks, the Culdees, 'lived by the work of their own hands', believing in a balance of three labours in each day – work for the mind, in teaching or reading – or, if there was a scriptorium, in copying; for the spirit in prayer, and a variety of physical tasks. We cannot be sure what they would have worn – a knee-length tunic, perhaps, as depicted in the cross-shaft from the ninth century, now stored in the chapel – but the later Augustinians, the Black Canons, would have fitted the stereotypical image of monks, with dark hooded cloak and long cassock lined with sheepskin over a linen surplice. And what of the monastery? The Book of Llandaff contains the Lives of two saints – Dyfrig and the hermit Elgar – exhumed in May 1120 and 'translated' to the new cathedral near Cardiff, in which the topography of the island is sketched: 'the dominating headland of the eastern shore and the level and fertile pasture of the western – damp with sweet flowing springs and the sea-shore full of dolphins, but free from any snake or frog', but without any detail of how or where the monks lived. There are snippets about pirate raids, occasional names of benefactors and agents, a pardon to the Abbot for supporting Owain Glyndŵr's rebellion, and a handful of references to the island's sanctity in medieval Welsh poetry – and one sarcastic attack on the Abbot for poor hospitality offered to a fifteenth-century travelling bard, Deio ap Ieuan Ddu, in his *Ode of the Cheese*. Nothing to bring the place itself into focus. At Penmon in Anglesey, the site of the third ancient monastery of Wales, there is an illustration of the layout of church and cloister, guest house, infirmary, barns and store-sheds, a 'necessarium' or privy, and a 'warming room' – a nice touch on an island often wet and windy – all enclosed by a wall or earth bank for shelter and protection. There was more change and disturbance, a growing population, on Bardsey. 'A long stone building' is described by Pennant in 1778 as 'the Abbot's house, still inhabited by several of the natives', along with 'a singular chapel or oratory' and from about 1480 there is a mention of stained glass in the church – but poets' fancy is not always to be trusted, and Thomas Kelli, who portrays the island as a garden of Eden visited by God, is no exception.

When I asked Gwen about the change from an independent monastery to an organised order under formal rule, the big change in 1252, she said, rather apologetically, 'I'm only fired by the ancient ones, really. Did you know that the period known in English history as the Dark Ages is our Welsh Age of the Saints?' (Writing this, I am reminded how she spoke of Cadfan and Lleuddad as easily and affectionately as if they had been favourite uncles.) The keenest authority on the rise and fall of what became St Mary's Abbey of Bardsey was Mary Chitty, whom I'd met among that church group who came to Hendy in 1968 and who maintained her acquaintance with the island for the rest of her life. Where Gwen glowed and exclaimed, Mary was clear and cool, a woman of integrity silver as her hair, a scholar to her fingertips. She too loved the island, and with the sureness of a respected archaeologist and historian, explored the primary sources deciphering 'the dreadful mess' of ancient documents, puzzling out Latin and inconsistent medieval spelling between folds and stains. Fortunately she was persuaded to organise what she called her 'historical scrapbook' into two small books,

The Monks of Ynys Enlli, Parts I and II. The last was published on her ninety-fifth birthday. Privately printed, they are still available, locally and from her daughter: no better to be found.

Mary showed me copies of letters dated August 2nd, 1284, 'from Bardsey', when St Mary's Abbey was important enough to justify a royal visit from Edward I. Despite Norse raids in the ninth and tenth centuries (in 857 the Vikings had over a hundred ships off Dublin, less than fifty miles away), the monks had persisted; they had come back to mend or rebuild, and reclaim eminence. So for three days the island was effectively the seat of English government, with twenty shiploads of personal servants and trusted notables accommodated in tents. Treasury accounts of 1284 note payments to a team of 25 'tentmen' and 4 carpenters, plus two boys to clear nettles and thorns. One donation of twenty-eight shillings is recorded, and another, from Queen Eleanor's purse, of 19 pence. On the strength of this visit, the Abbey was able to continue building, and the tower that still stands was built about this time.

This was the heyday of the island's fame, and encouraged by the Pope's declaration that three pilgrimages to Bardsey was the equivalent of one to Rome, ensured prosperity for the next two hundred and fifty years.

Dissolution

It sounds gentle, a gradual absorption into the landscape; a clever name for an act of barefaced power. The King, Henry VIII, broke with the Church of Rome and his sweeping reforms were designed to wipe out Catholic practices: pilgrimages and saying the Mass were banned, monasteries and nunneries were destroyed and the inmates turned out. By 1537 this destruction reached further than the plague had done, to the very end of Llŷn and to Bardsey itself. Even if there were only a few monks left by then, as at Beddgelert, a certain amount of violence must have been involved, if only to the buildings: 'the Church hows and steple ben defac'd, having neither belles leade iron nor glas remayninge upon the same. And there is no habytacioun in the said Ile' reads a survey of 1547 (albeit possibly the author was the tenant himself who wished to paint a picture of worthlessness). There was, he pointed out, 'no kynde of woode, no pasture, arable or medow grownd within yt by reson of the grete plentye of conyes (rabbits)'. Only forty years before there had been a priory, barns, orchards and gardens and funds enough to send the Abbot, John Conway, on pilgrimage himself, to Rome.

All that is left of Bardsey's famous monastic past is the ruined thirteenth-century building we call 'the Abbey tower', a decorated floor tile from this period now in the British Museum, and a handful of objects now all lost or retained by their finders. These include: a silver crosier 'in the shape of a hand and arm', a ring and seal and a gold noble of Edward III reported in *Archaeologia Cambrensis*; more gold coins found near Carreg in 1846; and, in recent years, a 'grave penny', apparently a rare King Edgar coin from the ninth century found on a dig organized by Lampeter University when about thirty skeletons were discovered in Tŷ Newydd and removed from the island.

Bardsey and its *demesne* on the mainland (Cwrt and much of present-day Uwchmynydd – all the other churches, lands, granges and mills were ceded separately) was given to a variety of owners until, in 1553, it was awarded to John Wyn ap Huw of Bodfel. He – or his son of the same name – was arraigned in Star Chamber sixteen years later for being 'chief captaine of the pirates at Bardsey', harbouring brigands here, and supplying their ships with beef, beer and stores. He died in his bed, however, and his Wynn descendants, the Lords Newborough, owned the island for more than four hundred years.

Throughout that time it is likely that families lived here, tending the cattle and the 'wild men'. Some of the older names may carry echoes of this period. Ogof Lladron (pirates' cave) is a deep gully which may have been a high, deep cave where a ship could hide, the roof fallen and shattered into the many boulders that now litter its base. Another 'gut' is called Ogof Morgan; one old story says this is where the famous pirate captain came ashore to hide his treasure, but it's more likely to be a folk memory of the William Morgan, employed as overseer of the island, 'who aided and encouraged the visits of these lawbreakers by supplying all their needs of water and food and supervising the disposal of the illegal goods to distant markets'. Trwyn Dihyryn testifies to some sort of rogue, and Twll Halen (Salt Hole) perhaps to smuggled supplies at a time when it was taxed at £12 a ton.

In the seventeenth century the Irish Sea was a lawless place, 'an hot potch of brigands of all nations in Europe' according to Captain Richard Plumleigh, master of the government ship *Antelope*, sent to harry pirates and gun-runners. In 1625, Lundy had been captured and all its inhabitants taken off as captives for ransom. Merchants came from as far away as Bristol to Pwllheli, well-known as a place to pick up wines, sugar, silks, olive oil and even tea and tobacco: some of these may have been contraband stored on Bardsey.

The basis for the later thriving agricultural community was laid down then, in Bardsey's Dark Age, possibly in descendants of the monks' labourers who might have stayed on or returned after the King's men had left the area. There were undoubtedly tenants living there in 1646: the owner Colonel John Bodfel, trying to claim independence for the island, presents a statement from two of them testifying that they had always been 'free and quitte from ye paim't of any mize, taxation or other imposicion'. His summing-up rather spoils his case: 'It is a small poor island. It is not in Caernarvonshire but in Pembrokeshire or some other shire as some say.' (No rates were levied on island properties, however, until the late Sixties, a fact that is always quoted with apparent awe by any traveller or newspaper account.)

In the English Civil War Bardsey was strategically important: Cromwell was fighting in Ireland too, and a naval signalling station may have been built just below the summit of the mountain. A royalist ship attempted to seize the island in 1649, landing soldiers in Solfach (imagination provides flashes of musket fire between the rocks on a foggy night) but the garrison of Commonwealth forces (under a Lieutenant Aspinall) not only fought off the attack but captured the troops. I was excited to find bills 'for iron and work for securing the prison' and for 'transporting prisoners to Caernarfon' a couple of years later. In 1662 the island was visited by its first naturalist John Ray, who reported on birds and plants implying farming activities, and the great number of 'puffins' – a name used then for the Manx shearwaters. He mentions a ruined church, adding, 'three more they told us of'.

In the next century the island was passed between different owners in a flurry of leases, mortgages and easements, but by 1773 Thomas Wynn, 1st Baron Newborough was firmly back in possession and with his young second wife Maria Stella took a new interest in the place. A survey was made of all his property. When I was researching, I was lucky enough to be invited into the Glynllifon Estate Office to examine the finely-drawn maps, each field numbered, and the fine copperplate script. The most obvious difference is in the road and the landing-place. It was about this time that Thomas Pennant landed here, 'in a little sandy creek', as he puts it, after going round the South End, and it is clear that Solfach was the only safe place to come ashore then.

There were about sixty people living in four 'quarters': Groes, Christian, Bengen and Penthryn, each paying rent of £20 a year. Working back from census records and gravestones, individual islanders started to come into focus, with names and dates and traceable offspring. There were several generations of people born on the island and living their whole lives here, in a dozen dwellings clustered in the shelter of the mountain, small houses, probably not unlike Carreg Bach today but with turf roofs. Some lived in 'the abbot's house, a large stone building occupied by several of the natives' and 'not far from it . . . a singular chapel, or oratory, being a long arched edifice, with an insulated stone altar near the east end' (Fenton's *Tours of Wales*, 1814). In 1776 there were dairy cows and calves, poultry, many pigs, 'rearing stock' (probably young cattle) and 20 horses, needed more than anything for the heavy work of carting seaweed to the fields as fertilizer.

Oatmeal was a staple food. Bread was made from the barley grown on the island, roughly ground, and also used for brewing: hops were plentiful. Meat and fish were salted and dried. The women boiled up potatoes and kelp to make soap; they dipped peeled rushes into tallow – melted fat, perhaps from seals – for candles; there was a carpenter who could also make clogs; they would spin and weave woollen cloth, but for flannel – and for tea and sugar – they had to cross the Sound.

81

Island in the Current

Fishing has always been important to the islanders: Thomas Pennant testifies to it. The reputation of the Bardsey men as skilful seamen began in the eighteenth century, during the great herring glut, when they traded salt fish from the smaller ports of Llŷn, sailing out far west to meet boats putting out from the Irish coast. It would not be surprising if they brought back heavily-taxed goods, like salt, therefore becoming smugglers, but though there are many stories of ships coming to grief off the island, no stories of wrecking have been passed down, in contrast with mainland Llŷn: drenched sailors are saved, sometimes housed and fed for weeks on end until the storm dies down. The drowned are brought ashore, treated with the respect of those whose turn might come next, and settled into the earth decently, on the island or in Aberdaron churchyard. Only once did anyone try to make money out of this, and he was an islander only by marriage, and relative newcomer. Robert Williams had been turned out by his father the innkeeper of Gegin Fawr, the medieval hostelry in Aberdaron, for preaching temperance, so he came to live with the family at Hendy and began to take religious meetings in the chapel. He had a mixed reception from the islanders at first but there was a captive audience with little entertainment, and after he married Siân, the daughter of the house, acting as minister provided a useful supplement to the income from farming Hendy's sixteen acres. It appears that he saw a gap in the market for an island undertaker, too: there's a scrap of a scrawled bill in the archives:

July 1824   From Bardsey Island:

To Caernarfon	1-1-0d
For Catchit	5-0d
For send it cross and home back	10-0d
To Clerk	2-6d
For liquor and ale	3-0d
For coffin ....1- 0 -0d
Settled July 1824	3- 2-6d

Robert Williams

The sea provided, too. There must always have been competition for driftwood, *broc môr*, which I suppose means 'wreckage of the sea'. All sorts of things would have been tossed ashore by the tide: *The Life of Elgar* relates how the starving hermit discovered a freshly-dead stag on the beach. He feasted on it for a week. In 1822 the islanders had their first taste of oranges and lemons from the Azores when a vessel foundered with its cargo of 'ripe St Michaels' floating in all along the coast as far as Nefyn. Anything that was carried as ship cargo might find its way ashore and be claimed by the finder, either after shipwreck or just because it had fallen into the sea. Because of the lack of trees, timber was especially valuable, not just for firewood but also for repairs – a good straight piece to lash a broken mast, for instance – or for fencing, or for shelves or even more sophisticated furniture. When Ernest and I first set up home on the island, we inherited a *chaise longue* with elegant bendy legs, made out of *broc* in the Thirties, a period described by Ronald Lockley in *I Know an Island*. He observed the urgency of harvesting the driftwood. Returning from an all-night vigil birding at the lighthouse, he would find one or other of the farmers' sons ranging the beach in the half-light before dawn: 'There is a wonderfully healthy competition in the hunt for driftwood, in which the rule is that the first man to throw a plank on the greensward gets it. Anything larger than a pencil is eagerly snapped up.' Children were sometimes sent to the shore to watch a particular prize as it came nearer on the tide; Brenda Chamberlain's partner, Jean 'The Frenchman' trained his sheepdog to leap into the water and nudge floating planks into shore so that he could grab them first and, by dragging them above high water mark, lay claim to them according to island custom.

Even more crucial items depended on the sea's gifts. 'An islander without his own boat is unthinkable,' said Lockley, and each family here would have had its own craft, at least a dinghy for lifting a few lobster pots or going out in the bay to catch a mackerel or pollack for supper. For crossing to the mainland, something bigger and more robust was needed: it is after all five and a half miles to Porth Meudwy, the nearest landing-place, and the Sound notoriously dangerous. In 1822 Trinity House equipped their boatman with a former ship's lifeboat, the *Supply*, and it was probably then that the custom of a shared

83

'island boat' started. The landlord, Lord Newborough, after repeated entreaties, gave a ship's lifeboat, the *Ynys Enlli,* to the islanders on condition that they contributed towards its upkeep (three shillings and sixpence for every pound of rent) but by the Twenties it was in poor shape and its 'modern paraffin engine' was notoriously unreliable. Yet the capital investment for a big boat for livestock, supplies, passengers and all was out of reach of the tenants. Wil's fishing boat *Gwen* was built out of driftwood at a time when he couldn't have afforded anything else, and then, in the early years of the Second World War, he picked up first the nameplate off a wrecked boat (*Benlli)* and then some weeks later, an old ship's lifeboat drifting off Pen Diban. With skilled woodwork and a new engine, *Benlli* – 'the old Benlli' – became the island's lifeline, and when there was enough cash to order the building of a brand-new boat in the Sixties, that was named *Benlli II.* Forty years later the boat that carries visitors to Bardsey, built and skippered by Wil's grandson, Colin – my son – is named with an almost superstitious reverence *Benlli III.* But she is bright yellow fibreglass, not overlapping planks of larch on an oak keel.

The sea has always been highway and workplace for Bardsey men. Until modern times, travel overland was slow and dangerous – the risks of highway robbery often outweighing those of rough seas and fickle weather. We forget how muddy unpaved roads would be for half the year; how rough and dusty the rest. In lawless times, the reputation of the crossing and the treacherous overfalls of Gorffrydiau Caswennan – the submerged rock that once wrecked Arthur's ship the *Gwennan*, as legend told it – kept the curious away. Then as now, the islandmen knew the tides and the moods of the sea, and rode them. Yes, billions of tons of water surge in and out through the Sound, most hazardous when wind runs against tide. But currents can be used – a favourable flood-tide will sweep a boat along as fast as a small outboard engine.

There were six 'big boats' on the island in the 1770s, used for taking island produce – oysters, seed-corn, butter – to Liverpool. The wooden 'sweeps' used to row the last of these boats have been stored across the beams in the barn at Nant. Each is fifteen feet long. 'In those days,' reported Thomas Jones, in *Tomos o Enlli,* 'all the Enlli men were strong. Their arms were as stout as the waists of ordinary men.' Many boys of Bardsey

from Broc Môr

Mornings, still, the islanders 'walk round',
working the shore for a first finding
of what high tide has left them.
Once, ranked on the rocks hours-long
they'd wait or post children to watch
to make sure of a cask or hefty plank.
In rivalry or spite sometimes they'd wade
or, boots and all, leap wide into the swell.
Dim, the Frenchman's sheepdog, did a sea-fetch,
trained to nose good pickings safe ashore.

The sea provided: a barrel bursting butter
sweating salt; sea-moulded lumps
of dark wax I still polish with; the captain's chair
at the head of our table; wrecked and waterlogged
the boat and then its nameplate *Benlli*
homing in on echoes to Caswennan; a mask
hung slit-eyed by the fire to send Tŷ Pella kids
shrieking to bed; Arthur's clogs, the left
picked up in March, its match two months later.
Once on the Narrows a whole ash tree
trunk wide as a table, bur riddled with shipworm,
generations of voyagers. In wartime
grey barrels bobbing in like schools of whales
found full of still-sweet water. And a real whale,
mine-mutilated, stinking in Traeth Ffynnon.

stock made staunch sea captains. Not surprising, then, that they were threatened by press-gangs on their further trips, especially in Liverpool, as they reported to Lord Newborough, and on one occasion, on the island, betrayed by one of their own. Early in the Napoleonic Wars (begun in 1792), a naval vessel – 'a warship', the story says – anchored offshore and the men gathered round in their fishing boats to take a good look. They were invited aboard in a friendly manner. The only one who could speak English was Siôn Robert Griffith who, after a tot or two, was persuaded to sell the others – almost the entire male population – to the press officers. As he rowed ashore, the ship raised its anchor and sailed away south, with the men restrained below deck. When the women realised that none of their menfolk had returned from fishing, they went down to the beach in a body, to find only Siôn's boat pulled up on the shingle, and the others bobbing about some way off. They found him in the house where he was staying, hastily gathering his possessions, and when he boasted of what he'd done, their mood turned murderous. They dragged him outside, intent on a lynching, or worse, but he managed to get away from them and though they searched until dark, he stayed hidden in one of the many rocky gullies near Solfach until he could escape to the mainland and, with his ill-gotten fortune, take ship to America. He was never heard of again. Somehow the women got in touch with Lord Newborough's agent on the mainland – perhaps through the time-honoured custom of lighting a signal fire at the north end of the island – and through his intervention, the ship was intercepted and the men got back to the island in time for the harvest.

They had a king once

'The people of Bardsey have no incentive to fly to the mainland for shelter, for the coast is more inhospitable than the island where there is a good haven for boats. This, I think, makes the islanders the more contented with their home.' So Lockley suggested, recognising the difference between his own coast of Pembrokeshire, with its safe harbours, and the rocky shore of Llŷn. It is to Trinity House Lighthouse Corporation that the island owes its landing-place, the Cafn, or 'trough' created when they blasted through soft rock to make a new harbour. The nineteenth century was one of great change, even on Bardsey. It began with the building of the first chapel as part of the Great Awakening of Calvinistic Methodism, and then the slipway and the *storws* or boathouse during the construction of the lighthouse. The tower of limestone blocks, nearly a hundred feet high and unusually square, was completed in four months: the light was first 'exhibited' on Christmas Eve 1821. It is hard to imagine the effect on the islanders of what must have felt like an invasion of Cornish stonemasons and other workmen, of big ships anchored in the Bay and boats landing where previously had been nothing but perilous rocks; their whole perception of the place shifted south, and most dramatic of all, the night sky never to be dark again. Once in commission, the lighthouse was occupied by three keepers and their families, from places as foreign as the East End, Harwich, Devon, Northumberland, introducing varieties of English into the Welsh-speaking community. The harbour meant that coasters and the 'flats', cargo barges, could come in, and even, from mid-century, pleasure steamers from Aberystwyth and Caernarfon, disgorging as many as a hundred and twenty passengers. Opportunities for earning cash abounded – from employment with the lighthouse service to selling eggs and serving teas.

It was about this time that the Newborough family instigated the tradition of a 'King': it followed on from picnics where Lady Maria Stella presented ribbons for the assembled islanders' hats, and may have been a family joke. A crude tin crown was made (by a lighthouse keeper, as the story goes) and the King was crowned standing on a chair on a rise on the Narrows and holding a silver snuff-box. Only two kings were ever celebrated in this way: John Williams, who drowned in April 1841 leaving a one-day old son who was to become John Williams II. However, he is said to have drunk the rent money and ended up forced to leave the island, whereupon Love Pritchard of Tŷ Pella declared 'I am the oldest; I am going to be King now.'

It is sometimes said that the King was appointed to collect rents, but there was always a land-based agent who visited every year, and acted as go-between, although once Sir Spencer, 3rd Baron Newborough, inherited the title in 1833, islanders who could write sent letters direct to him. After the death of the first King his brother William

wrote on behalf of his sister-in-law, requesting that she be allowed to retain the Cristin tenancy; just six years later his wife, Ann Williams, Plas Bach, sent news that her husband had been lost on 22nd February. She apologised for the delay in writing, as she had been confined with her tenth child a week afterwards. She asked if she might keep the farm as all her children were at home and her eldest son would take charge.

Her husband's body was washed up in Aberdaron and is buried there:

> O rhoddi hwn mewn bedd oer bant
> Mae mam a phlant yn wylo
> (Putting this man in a cold, far grave
> Mother and children grieve.)

Ann Williams's letter was the start of a good relationship with his Lordship. He took a special interest in her family and stayed with them. Particular attention was paid to the design and construction of Plas Bach in the rebuilding, 'rooms were kept for his Lordship' with furniture brought from Glynllifon, and he had his own privy at the front of the house. Two of her sons were employed as sailors by him. In 1879 the doctor was fetched to Ann during a great storm – Wil had the story in vivid detail from the smithy – because she had an infection of the lungs, but she survived until Boxing Day 1886. Her will suggests a relatively rich woman, who had not relinquished control to her fifty-year-old sons of six horses, good numbers of cows, sheep and pigs, four carts and a boat. Her 'wearing apparel' was valued at £5 and her household furniture (excluding his Lordship's rooms) at ten.

I found another famous gravestone nearby, concerning the wreck of the *Supply*, a boat provided by Trinity House, which went aground in a thundery squall near the Cafn not long after the lighthouse was built. Six people were drowned, including the skipper's daughter who, it is said, had gone ashore to buy material for her wedding clothes. In a (lengthy) *Lament*, Ieuan Lleyn wrote of how her long dark hair floated like seaweed an arm's length out of reach of the islanders on what is still known as Trwyn y Fynwent (graveyard point) where six large stones were placed as memorials – until they were used in the building of the jetty in 1973.

Tide and wind carried the bodies out and across the Sound to the mainland.

> Underneath intered the body of Thomas Williams of Bardsey Island, Mariner aged 49. He perished in the execution of his duty as Master of the Bardsey Light Tender which was wrecked 30th of November 1822. This stone was here placed in testimony of his regard for the memory of the departed and his integrity by Joseph Goddard, Collr/ of H M Customs Caernarvon, and agent for the Bardsey Light, also the remains of Sydney, daughter of the above Thomas Williams, aged 20, who lost her life on this same melancholy occasion.

Thomas Jones looks back to those times in *Tomos o Enlli* and a generation later Sudne Ward-Jones, née Williams of Plas Bach – a descendant – told me how the *hen bobl* felt:

> We were like one body . . . yes, there were disagreements, usually over very little things; my goodness, times when you really hated somebody or other, but there was no choice, it was like falling out with your own sister or cousin, you can't carry on without them. So the quarrel was put aside and life went on. You needed your neighbours; we all had to work together, whether we liked it or not. And there were all the old ones, the fathers and mothers, aunties and uncles and grandparents – even the dead and buried – they were all part of the family, too.

She was keen to emphasise how well they lived, dismissing any suggestion that they had ever needed to eat sea-birds' eggs. 'We had plenty of fowls – hens, duck, geese – the island is a perfect place for them, having no foxes. We had a good roast dinner every Sunday, and meat was never scarce.' There was home-killed lamb in autumn, and sometimes mutton; pork and bacon, cured in a big earthenware dish with molasses and several vigorous rubbings of salt; and once a year the butcher came to Plas Bach to kill a bullock, which would be shared out between all the households. Each of the ten farms she remembered set aside a field for growing potatoes, (first earlies like Sharpe's Express or Arran Pilot were planted in the sheltered gardens), carrots and swedes. Any surplus of these and other vegetables (shallots, lettuce, cabbage and peas) and fruit (rhubarb, gooseberries, apples) would be useful for the pigs. Bread was made from the barley grown on the island. The

corn – barley and oats – was threshed by hand with flails, and the cleaned grain taken to Aberdaron to the miller. Wheat flour (white bread flour) was bought in, in big sacks, but was considered a luxury until the twentieth century. 'Even when we couldn't cross to the mainland for six weeks all we were short of was flour – and baco for the men!' In the 1930s, the schoolteacher Mrs May Murray-Williams used to keep a store of tobacco to dole out to the men at such times 'to make things easier for the women'.

The islanders seemed to live much better than their counterparts on the mainland, or so it seemed to Nell Carreg who came from the mainland first as a child in 1910 and then returned as a young wife in 1926. In *Twenty-Six Years on Bardsey*, written by her daughter Bessie and translated from Welsh by Rosemary Gaches, she lists a typical day's meals: 'In the morning we would have oatmeal porridge for breakfast, or sometimes *brwas*. Then a thick slice of mam's good bread with butter and treacle.' (This remark reminded me of my mother-in-law's lifelong faith in eating *triog du* in the mornings as a remedy for all digestive ills.) 'For dinner, potatoes and meat or fish fresh from the sea. Fried or roasted, a proper dinner, with vegetables, like a Sunday dinner in Aberdaron. We didn't have much for tea in the afternoon, just a cup of something and a *tamaid*. Then for supper we had eggs and a big slice of bacon from a pig fattened on the island, that we'd salted ourselves. A ham hung from the ceiling in the *bwtri* and Mam cut slices just as she wanted them.'

Again, I hear Wil's voice: 'That home-cured bacon tasted like no other, and it didn't shrink in the pan, no water came out of it like the thin stuff you buy today.' Potatoes roasted with plenty of bacon rashers on top, and a huge dish of rice pudding yellow with cream was a perfect supper. And if anyone wanted a different taste, 'it was easy to get a rabbit. All we had to do was to go out to the fields with a ferret. In no time at all we would hear a great commotion down in the bowels of the earth and then the rabbit would shoot out as if fired by a gun and the dog would catch it in a twinkling.' The rabbit would be stuffed with sage and onion; or if it was a tough old buck, simmered slowly with leeks and carrots to make a tasty stew or a pie. Sixty years later, Mary Atkinson wrote in *Farmers' Weekly* how when they first came to Bardsey 'our staple was rabbit . . . I became quite expert in disguising it, but we've all had a sickener of it now.'

The living was good and the people prospered. There were several waves of emigration to America, young couples or whole families leaving in 1818, 1822, 1841 and 1881. Attempts were made to establish a school: in 1845, a young teacher came to the island, 'the schoolyn', who lodged with different families in turn, but the islanders had no money to pay him and after about five years he moved on. After the rebuilding of all the houses in the 1870s, fulfilling his vision of Bardsey as a model community, Lord Newborough paid a minister to take charge of the new chapel. He arrived in January 1879; the old self-appointed preacher Robert Williams (now quite prosperous, a ship-owner and a personage who liked to be taken for King on his mainland visits) died in April. W.T. Jones – titled the Missionary – was young and vigorous; he soon had a thriving Sunday School and taught the children for several hours each week, but also pestered the Education Department for a female teacher. The official reply was, as it was 'such an exceptional case', to offer a government grant of £15 a year plus an allowance of 12 shillings per head for each child, but only if the Missionary (or his wife) were willing to take a examination qualifying them for a fourth-grade certificate. This became the norm, a senior pupil sometimes invited to stay on past the leaving age of 14 as teaching assistant until the days of the resident minister passed, freeing Tŷ Capel, and from 1930 to 1950 a teacher was employed full time by the local authority, first Mrs May Murray-Williams, followed by Miss Menna Hughes, and finally, Mrs Sheltinga, or Dilys Cadwaldr as she was known from her column about island life in the *Cymro* and from winning the Prose Medal in the National Eisteddfod. At its busiest the School seems to have had no more than sixteen 'scholars' from the age of four to fourteen – with five from the lighthouse and six or seven from the Mission House, as it was called when William 'Enlli' Jones was minister and schoolteacher.

During the nineteenth century census records show the resident population was steady between 60 and 90 people, (rising on occasions when ships are present, for instance in 1881 when crews and even passengers of the *Sunlight,* the *Fiery Cross* and *Flamingo* were all included, 49 extra people) but the average age and the proportion of bachelors and spinsters can be seen to increase until in 1925 Love Pritchard told the *Daily Sketch*: 'We have not enough young men to row boats off for us and look after the cattle' under the headline *Life Too Dull: Why Bardsey is being deserted*. Among the 'boys' demand for modern ways' were the wireless and visits to the 'kinema'. And so (one feels almost pushed off by media pressure) the islanders decided to leave, 'to die among their kin' as one put it, in what was called the Exodus.

Rituals of the Good Life

In the autumn of 1931, Wil heard that Tŷ Pella might soon be vacant. It was what he had been waiting for. After the 'Exodus', all ten farms except Nant had been advertised and re-let to local families. His parents and his sister Lizzie Kate with her husband had taken the tenancy of both houses at Cristin and were doing well; it was a chance of your own farm, to make something of yourself, rather than being at a master's beck and call and scraping by on an agricultural labourer's wage. Early the following April, Wil and Nellie moved over to the island with their two-year-old daughter, Jane, their few bits of furniture and half a dozen hens. His parents gave them a cow and the cash to buy six sheep – Tŷ Pella at that time had 29 acres of fields and grazing rights on the mountain, one sheep for every pound of rent paid. 'But six was all we could afford, then,' Nellie told me once when we were surrounded by the din and jostle of ewes and lambs at shearing time.

When I began to spend my summers on Bardsey I had a lot to learn; not just a language (early on, I'd asked Ernest if he minded not speaking Welsh with me, and he'd replied that he'd always used both 'because of the lighthouse'), but there was a way of living, a sort of culture, to grow into as well. For my own mother, housework had been a drudgery she always resented, and so I'd never known how satisfying it could be to throw open windows to the sun or beat a carpet until its colours glowed. There was, I discovered, a way of doing things properly that could enhance the task and make one feel in touch with the generations who had evolved it. I learned weather signs and sayings: that an easterly wind blows by the hour but *gwynt gogledd wrth y dydd,* a northerly lasts all day; when it was best to plant potatoes, sow broad beans, set a hen to sit on a clutch of eggs (my father-in-law was particular about phases of the moon for all these things).

Folding laundered sheets, I found, had a pattern with steps as formal as a two-person dance. The linen must be held tightly at the corners with arms spread wide, pulled taut first straight and then diagonally before the edges were matched up and the sheet folded lengthwise once – to the senior person's right. Another stretch, and the dancers moved together to complete the folding. Vigorous smoothing on a flat surface took the place of ironing – on Bardsey at least, where the only tools were flat-irons heated on the hearth.

I learned the importance of a good hot stove. Ernest still swears that food cooked in the old paraffin oven tasted better, but trimming the wicks and filling it and all the lamps was the worst job, Nellie told me, because the smell of paraffin would linger on your hands all evening. And despite the noise of the generator, electricity was so much better to sew by; all those years of leaning close to the single candle or the lamp. But there was no friendliness in the new light, it was cold. The Tilley lamp gave as good a light, she thought, if you kept the pressure pumped up; yes, she missed the hiss and suck of the flame in its pearly mantle. It was company, like a fire. But one less job in the week's routine. If it was Monday, it was washing: suds boiling in the big cauldron over a fire of driftwood in the pig-kitchen, after feeding the yard beasts – calves, pigs, bottle-fed lambs – and the poultry (in 1940, according to a Ministry of Agriculture report, there were over 300 hens and ducks and 50 geese). Bread would have been kneaded and left to rise, three big loaves three times a week. There might be butter-making too: up until the death of Prince, the last cart-horse in 1956, using the horse-gin outside Cwt Llaeth, the dairy. And always, water to carry.

Each spring there would be the small ritual of cleaning the well, as generations of women have done from the beginnings of settlements near those places where water oozes from cracked stone. Nellie and I would gather our tools – a stiff hand-brush and a smaller scrubbing one; saucepans of decreasing size and then a tin, washed and polished to its original gleaming metal and crushed into a narrow pointy beak, to probe the deepest crevice. To lift the driftwood cover and dip into the gleaming water, at first shallowly so as not to disturb the sediment in the body of the well, then deeper, even to the bedrock, is to feel in touch with the deepest layers of occupation of a place, as if time had not passed, languages and beliefs and habits of living hardly changed. Human needs are the same, at least; the harvesting of water still a simple miracle if we think about it.

Free of the clogging shadows, and layers of mud, the well becomes something almost woken, a presence. We leave it for a day to fill, then go down with buckets. The water is cool on the hottest day, and seems to us more refreshing than tap or bottled stuff: it has a faint, mineral tang which I think is its memory of the rock that has filtered it. Each well on the island has a different taste: the best cup of tea is made from the hardest water, the kind that furs up the kettle with limescale.

Cleaning the well

Spindle of bubbles like blown breath
quivering the water, shape
of energy within the spring,
dances silver as we lift the lid.

Twelve buckets each to empty it
then countless scoopings of slick silt,
probing crevices where eels might live
scrubbing colour back into the stone.

Rose, ochre, malachite.
At the well-bed only fingers
can find the seep and feel a flow,
slow pulse from deep under.

Clearness oozes from cracked stone

So slow you cannot see it
the well re-fills; as if rock too
could unlock, quicken, swell, bring forth
a shining body in a bouncy skin.

It will take all night to fill,
a continuous generous offering
from the earth, and through us
back to the sea and the sky

it looks up to, vast white clouds
already beckoning on the horizon.
By morning it's an eye, wakeful
under its driftwood cover

waiting there among the gorse
for us to come with our buckets,
bend down to it, three silhouetted dolls,
who dip into its coolness, drink.

Taste the rock, the sea, the cloud.

Apocalyptic and After

It's hard to remember the shadow we lived under during the Cold War. It only seemed a matter of time before a nuclear attack – or a muddle – might wipe out the cities. How people might survive became a popular theme in novels like *Day of the Triffids* and *The Death of Grass;* there was a BBC TV serial and a magazine called *The Survivalist.* It was in this atmosphere of frozen terror in the early Seventies that John Griffiths thought of buying Bardsey to set up a survival community. After almost four hundred years of ownership, the Newborough family had been forced to put the island on the market to pay death duties.

An energetic entrepreneur and writer (with a special interest in science fiction), Griffiths had a well-worked out plan to create a community of twenty to thirty residents financed by an upmarket timeshare scheme aimed at jaded businessmen. It included a restaurant for dining on island-produced food, a small golf-course, wind-generators, possibly an airstrip on the Narrows. The first thing was to secure a reliable water supply for all the houses and their ensuite facilities (some already had these, but they fitted underneath the beds). Water engineers from London were brought in to do a survey and recommended a huge reservoir to collect the overflow from the wells behind Nant. It would be dug into the ground and well covered with earth, for both aesthetic reasons and to avoid contamination by radioactive fall-out. Next was making sure of getting there. 'How much would you like for a boat that will cross in all weathers?' he asked Ernest. 'Can't be done,' was the reply. 'But if money's no object, surely . . .' This time there was a slight pause, then a decisive shake of the head. 'You might cross in a lifeboat in a big sea, but then you wouldn't be able to land . . .'

It was a heady time, the prospect of having the money and the interest to turn Bardsey back into a bustling, self-sufficient place. The plans for converting the buildings were exciting and ingenious. There were reservations, though. Such bold plans were a bit suspect; nothing like them had ever been thought of, locally. Wil sucked on his pipe and said little; Nellie sniffed and looked out to sea as though there was something interesting on the horizon. They should have been honoured to be selected as the only couple beyond child-bearing age, like the Noah and Mrs Noah of a new world. I was fascinated by the idea, by how a group of strangers with nothing in common might weld into a community, and appalled at the possibility of a machine-gun emplacement on Pen Cristin and a selective breeding programme, if the worst happened. Did I want to survive, to bring children into such a world? John got as far as appointing his manager couple, a farmer and a full-time gardener, designing a colourful brochure and deciding on a colour scheme for the houses based on the island's palette ('all soft greens and greys, with touches of brilliant yellow and heather') when his offer was gazumped and Bardsey sold to a more acceptable fellow member of the aristocracy.

There was some publicity as the sale went through, for the newspapers picked up on a story that the 'English Lord' intended to prevent all access and keep the island as a private retreat. Whatever his longer-term plans, the new owner, now Lord Cowdray, generously offered Wil and Nellie the school as a courtesy let for as long as they wanted and allowed Sister Helen Mary, the Anglican hermit from Oxford, to stay on in her loft at Carreg. She actually began to extend her territory to the other outbuildings and to create a garden plot by digging up the cobbled farmyard and laboriously carting topsoil in an old pram she found. The Bird Observatory, started in 1953 and the only one in Wales, continued at Cristin and a new tenant for the farm was sought. By luck, our connection with Bardsey was maintained: Ernest and I had the chance of Dynogoch, the house next door to his lifelong home, because the new farmers, Jane and Arthur Strick, appreciated help with the boats. 'Bardsey's the place for you,' they had been told by a lighthouse-keeper with happy memories of the island. If they wanted independence and a good life, they'd find it there, he assured them. In April 1972 the Stricks decided to give it a try. They travelled up from Devon in a Land-Rover towing a horsebox of animals, crossed to the island with Ernest the following day and stayed twenty-two years.

They found their new home as described: more sheltered at the heart of the Irish Sea, a gentler landscape than the high, windswept plateau of Lundy where they had lived for thirteen years; the farmland more fertile, and much nearer to the mainland. Despite this it was more difficult to get to, they found, than Lundy, which had a regular boat service out of Ilfracombe bringing supplies and tourists and a lively social life centred on the pub. What was harder about living on Bardsey, Arthur found, was coping with the mainland as well – crossing to Aberdaron to sell lobsters and shop for everything needed, fence-posts and sheep medicines, bottled gas and food.

I ask Jane what she thought it was that gave them the staying power, for they must have been among the most solitary of Bardsey's inhabitants. The young couple who had come with them left after a few months, and another who thought well-paid jobs might be well lost for island freedom lasted barely two years. Once the lighthouse had been made automatic and the keepers were withdrawn, Jane was completely alone whenever Arthur crossed to the mainland for stores.

'We were mostly too busy to think about it,' she replies. 'There was always so much to do, so much to learn. We were greenhorns, really, at farming. Of course, I'd helped with the ponies on Lundy, and with lambing but never coped on my own, and so I was there, almost book in one hand and the poor sheep in the other . . . Wil and Nellie were wonderful, they never intruded but were always ready to help.'

'And I had a lot to learn about the boat,' Arthur puts in. 'I'd handled small boats round Lundy, of course, ferrying stuff ashore and lifting a few lobster pots, but the *Benlli* was a lot bigger than what I was used to, and I had to learn the ways across the Sound and all about the tides and currents.'

After an initial injection of capital in the farm, the owner's enthusiasms switched elsewhere and the island began to sink into a gentle decay. Wind and weather began to unpick the houses, slate by slate, and window panes gaped empty. At the North End, stable doors hung off their hinges and nettles flooded the farmyards. There were few fences, and sheep roamed everywhere. How betrayed the old people must have felt a hundred years before when their sons and daughters had left and they had to watch fields they had worked all their lives go back to marshland and thistle.

Then the 'Romantic Island Retreat, Two Hours from London by air . . . with consent for a Residence' was on the market again. This time people who cared about the island didn't stand back. The Bardsey Island Trust was formed and after a passionate fund-raising campaign 'to salvage what is left of the traditional way of life of this unique Welsh community' was able to 'secure' the island in 1979 and to start restoration work. People started to come back to the Observatory and for summer holidays. The Trust employed an estate worker, a housekeeper and a gardener, as well as an Island Manager. The Stricks' sheep did well on the fertile land, and Jane made the Bardsey name famous again through her prize-winning Connemara ponies. Their island breeding made them hardy and sure-footed, and Bardsey Promise was particularly successful, becoming Reserve Champion of all the breeds at Olympia.

After Arthur had to have a hip replacement, people started telling them, 'You're getting too old for the life you lead,' people started telling them, and so they made the decision to retire to a smallholding on the mainland. 'I've never regretted coming off when we did,' Jane says. 'It was the right time. And I'm glad we lived there before there were too many restrictions and all the paperwork connected with farming these days.' Of course, Arthur misses the sea, but not the daily struggle with it. For it is hard, even now, to make a living on Bardsey. Lifting lobster pots is heavy work in an often hostile and unreliable environment: many days and gear are lost when it is too rough to go out. Farming can be frustrating: you get lambs ready for market and then the weather turns so you can't get them off for three weeks. Start cutting hay and a pin breaks on the mower and can't be replaced for ten days. A cow falls over the cliff and there's no way anyone can get to her, not even a RAF rescue helicopter because it's too stormy, and she's washed off the rocks. 'The main thing Bardsey taught us,' Jane sums up, 'is to be phlegmatic. There's nothing you can do about the weather, you just have to wait until things get better. If you can't sort it yourselves, you have to put up with it. The worst thing was not being able to get the vet across when animals were in trouble.'

Back in the Seventies, Ernest had been offered the farm tenancy but he had always said 'One farmer can't manage.' He knew the effort involved in bringing everything to the island and coping with the demands of the farm and lobster-fishing. He had grown up with the ever-present gap between time and work to be done; as demand for a boat service grew, shearing or haymaking dragged out over weeks, and where he wanted to be was on the sea. Jane and Arthur had coped by hiring in specialist help, for instance a gang of shearers and students to help with lambing, and by inviting those staying on the island to help: returning visitors reminisce about sheep-drives and working in the hayfields with wooden rake and pitchfork. They are disappointed to see the baler. After the Stricks, a consortium of three young locals farmed the island, employing a shepherd to live year-round at Tŷ Pella, now synonymous with 'The Farm'. Tim was an agriculture student at Aberystwyth who had learned Welsh as part of his dream of having his own farm in Wales, and especially, on Bardsey. For him and Dot (they were married by special licence on the island) this was a beginning, an opportunity to practise the skills of self-sufficiency they have continued to live by on the mainland. Those were happy times, especially when their baby son Iestyn was born.

Castaways Wanted

It might have been Ronald Lockley who started the idea of 'getting away from it all' to Bardsey, visiting in 1938 'as ambassador' of the young people who had written to him

99

after he had started describing his life on Skokholm in *The Countryman* magazine. 'They wanted to know if they could get out of the cities . . . (for) an island autonomy where modern luxuries could be exchanged for the freedom to think and do in the fresh air and to live by home-produced goods. I knew Bardsey supported a community which lived as near this way as any other I had heard of . . .' As a result of Lockley's essay 'John Evans and the Good Life', a young merchant seaman called Eddie Roberts came to farm at Tŷ Nesaf. Resourceful and eager to learn, he soon settled into island life and married Wil and Nellie's daughter, the Jane I had talked with in the school on my first visit.

The island has offered sanctuary in the past, perhaps been a hiding-place, but as anyone who spends anything more than a holiday there will discover, people bring their own problems and there is no escape. In winter especially it takes a strong relationship to survive months with hardly anyone else to talk to and without the distractions of going out, buying things, libraries, food in the daily variety we now expect, broadband . . . even radio if the batteries run out. Then more than ever the island becomes a magnifying glass for emotions. In the itch of the solitary mind, especially, there is no relief. *Madman Runs Berserk in Lonely Lighthouse* screams a headline from 1959, describing the breakdown of a man trying to spend the winter as a hermit. He is not the only one to have 'lost it', needing to be brought off, sometimes by RAF helicopter. It has become a sort of convention with the Bardsey Island Trust that to live on the island all year round now without the support of a community, a partner is necessary.

In 2000, the farm tenancy was advertised like a reality TV show: *Castaways shortlist for island challenge* reported the *Liverpool Daily Post*. Though *The Guardian* reported 'more than 1,100 people are interested' only one person with any farming experience applied, just ten forms were returned and two couples and one single man interviewed. Dave and Libby Barnden arrived on the island in September 2001 accompanied by a film crew and had photographers for magazines such as *Hello!* flying across the Atlantic to snap them against a backdrop of sparkling sea. However, they and the old ewes they had bought settled in well and despite problems with Libby's health and education for their two teenage daughters, there were five good years.

Now the island is farmed by a local man, Gareth Roberts from Cwrt, with input from the RSPB and with a shepherd/stockman resident at Tŷ Pella. The Porter family – who already knew the place well, keeping bees here – have just come through their first winter, a particularly stormy one, but Steve and Jo and their two children are full of enthusiasm and plans for the future. I envy Rachel and Ben, and five-year-old Connor at the Observatory, growing up with the sea all around them and, even in storm, that deep sense of belonging that is a kind of safety. Perhaps they will develop that true quality of islanders, tenacity. One of Wil's favourite sayings was 'Keep at a job, it will get done sometime.'

I hope I may have acquired some by proximity, for through many changes we have maintained our link with the island, have hung on to the house so that our sense of identity is caught up in it. If I feel that, how much stronger it must be in Ernest, for whom it was truly the world until he started venturing in his late teens; he had really been nowhere else – and the others for whom all their growing, even before birth, was accompanied by the fog-horn, the sea murmuring or roaring, the seals' voices lifted at low tide, the shearwaters homing in thick dark. And through these years I have been standing by, witnessing the end of a way of life that has persisted for hundreds of generations. For we only play at it really. Sheltering by the Stone Age midden near Solfach or striding through the teeth of a gale past where the Viking long-house may have stood on Penrhyn Gogor, I shiver at the thought of living then, surviving by wearing skins and eating limpets in hard times. Luckily for me, while I carry water from the well or scrub jeans outside on a slate slab, I know that in October I will be able to pick up the comforts and conveniences of twenty-first century living again: washing machines, supermarkets, email and television. I will happily take part once more in mock-migrations, self-centred pilgrimages, by car or plane. In the lifetime of stories Wil told me, change is the one constant of our lives. What humans do best is adapting our environment; we make places significant by living in them generation to generation. We can re-invent them, but we cannot keep them as they are. And the truth is, they belong to no one; none of us will leave much of a mark.

from Vespers

The pulse of this place: weather wings
the stumbling, persistent hum
of bees in late-flowering heather
and plainsong, pacing footsteps;
it is the swish, the shiver and fall
of the swathe to the scythe,
and dry stutter of tractors
and the white mare's hour-long tramp
round the horse-gin, the thwock and splash
of butter coming; chapel bell
and foghorn
and the shipping forecast
three times a day; diesel-throb that turns
the light held level in its bath of mercury;
the swing of waves and the surge and tick
of young in the womb,
the push of men and the trudge of women
carrying milk, carrying water, carrying wood and children
born and unborn.

Nellie gathering her washing from the gorse
behind the school hoods a hand over her eyes
to scan the south-west
for tomorrow's weather. For the sixtieth year
she calculates the springs' slow drying,
the readiness of hay, what men and boys
are still at sea, though there is no one now
she has to keep the kettle hot for. She remembers
out at five to help Wil push the *Gwen,*

elvers wriggling between her toes
the child dancing on the limekiln in her nightie
when she got back; walking with her
to find the cows (if only they would stand
for milking); carrying the skim
to the calves in Plas, water to the bull,
boiled potatoes to the styed pig. Running
to chase the cats from crocks of ripening cream.
Churning. Baking. Scrubbing and washing and mending
food on the table five times a day
and in the evening, steps in the yard
click of the latch and a lighthouse-keeper
for company till his watch at midnight.

It holds the sea in the crook of its arm,
this island, blending and letting
difference shine: the gaudy barber's pole
of the lighthouse, the new boat's bird-yellow
beckoning the eye to the *storws* roof
brocaded with lichen. For generations
the driftwood door's been shut
only when all the boats are safely home.
Inside, old rope hibernates in lazy coils.

Seals grunt and mutter and exult, a congregation
getting the *hwyl*, with the cries
of gulls and lambs and Cristin children
playing in the hour before they sleep.

Чуул ев з ругала
Сео.

horizons

Inside the Lens

It is spring, a sparkling morning with a north-westerly breeze chivvying high cloud. To stand inside the lens in the lantern in the lighthouse tower and look out is to watch the world turn slowly in a kaleidoscope of blue and silver, grey-green or rusty bracken red.

I look around as if getting my bearings: this feels like a new place. In the polished windows, ghostly reflections of the prisms turn and wheel, the sun is stretched and splinted into points like a Christmas tree star. The floor, a flanged steel platform that supports the great lens as it floats in its bath of liquid mercury, flickers with patterned segments of shadow that print my arms and hands as well. Behind me, the light bulb is outsize, but not dazzling; domestic, placid at the heart of its five-sided cage. It is a pentagon, I realise, where a net of sunlight holds me at the centre. Clumsy as an old-fashioned diver's helmet from outside, the louvred panels curving round me become a cocoon. Close up, the whorls of glass petals do not have the sheeny translucence of windows; their thickness has set them cloudy as wax. Some refract the light, some reflect; some magnify and others are shaped to reduce and focus. From a distance it might seem a Cyclops eye but of course it is not a lens for looking through: it is an assemblage of prisms for gathering light and broadcasting it out over the sea as a signal, a beacon with its own individual signature to read and work out where you are on a journey. It could be a metaphor for the role Bardsey has played in human consciousness from time immemorial.

The familiar view is alive with movement. The mountain runs like water, a green wave rising only to dribble away, while sky sways and rolls, sometimes upside down so it's hard to tell which is sea and which blue air, all constantly fragmenting and re-forming between glimpses of rainbow. But even as a jumbling mosaic, the island's shape holds steady, recognisable. So many people who come here look at it through lenses – binoculars, telescopes, cameras – and always, even in the distant past, those of their own expectations.

What I see has changed little in forty years but the way I see it has. A line of Wordsworth intones itself in memory: 'not as in the hour of thoughtless youth . . .' As I walk the island these days I feel an increasing sense of what he called 'something far more deeply interfus'd'; some meaning for which the key is mislaid, a message in a language whose alphabet we may have forgotten. Something to do with perspective, perhaps. Just as we have learned to see the earth as a bright jewel hanging in space and to appreciate what a fragile film of atmosphere we have to live in, I think we'll come to sense how small a pocket of time we inhabit. What we see as a long history is only the top layer, infinitesimally thin and temporary – a sea-bed of the future. Except that the past here doesn't feel drowned and gone: rather it is as though different presents go on flowing, like the currents that gave the island its original name in Welsh, *ynys yn y lli.* Those swirls and eddies move at different speeds and depths, one riding dominant until the muscular ripple of the next catches the light, before that, too, plunges under in a continuous churning and recycling.

A sense of other lives often rises on Bardsey, all the stronger perhaps for the lack of physical waymarks. Sitting on the rocky shelves at Bae Nant, imagination reaches back for what it might have been like for a medieval pilgrim stepping ashore, itchy with lice, probably hungry, parched, footsore, perhaps sickening already or crippled with rheumatism; or for the earlier hermits, half-starved and deranged by loneliness so that they saw dead saints flickering like flame in the air; those eighteenth-century fishermen for whom it was the world, returning after being press-ganged into the Napoleonic War; for the farm-wives a century later trapped in relentless routines and carrying wood, carrying water, carrying children, born and unborn. Did they envy sisters in Pwllheli or

Liverpool stepping out round the shops or meeting new friends at chapel? Some of them hardly ever set foot in a boat. My mother-in-law crossed the Sound so rarely that even the thought of it could make her seasick.

Whatever the difficulties of getting here, however wet or uncomfortable the crossing, people always say that as soon as you set foot on the island, the place takes over. Wind and ozone set senses tingling: huge skies, far hills and coast-lines, the vast and living sea, but intimate particularity engages as well – I catch myself gazing for minutes on end at yellow lichen on a stone or a shield bug scuttling in the grass, as a child will stare in wonder at a worm. Individual details, given attention, take on the power of symbols. A star ten million years old, a single scarlet pimpernel in the potato patch, a leaf-cutter bee emerging from the nest it has bored in a driftwood bench, each silver striation of the timber. It is the nearest I get to what the Buddhists call 'sitting' in meditation: getting away from the narrow, grasping self in a contemplation of 'the other', which is everything else. Awareness deepens. This, I believe, is where all faiths spring from; it may also be an echo of what it has cost to become human and self-conscious, that sense of oneness and of inclusion experienced only intermittently in a lifetime.

I love – yes, it's not too strong a word, not just gush – I love being here because of that feeling of losing myself in impressions: the timelessness that comes from floating immersed in the moment. On all but the calmest days the air is moving around the island and there is the sound of the sea, like breathing, its movement and that of the light on it, encircling. Cloudscapes are richer, and more dramatic: the sky dominates the view and we lie in the path of all the weather from the south-west. As it streams across, the wind lifts and heaps cumulus clouds so that they dance, transforming as if in exhilaration, or whips cirrus into strands called *blew geifr*, goats' hair. Inland and in cities I have felt trapped beneath the weather, thick layers of grey, but here even heavy cloud is illuminated from below by light thrown back by the sea. When the sky darkens with approaching thunder, the air trembles as though a train is speeding onward; and in a real gale, so strong it's possible to lean on the wind, the storm goes roaring past, indifferent as a great machine, which is, I suppose, what the planet's weather system is.

Afterwards in the dramatic gullies beyond the lighthouse the sea will send up plumes of water that explode into white spray. Depth charges in reverse, they leave the chasms brimming with foam.

No wonder Bardsey attracts artists: it is impossible to spend any time here without being aware of the many qualities of light. Walking the shore I note how, in the deep, steep-sided coves, sunlight seems to dive straight down and lie on the bottom, quivering, like a luminous fish. It can be fierce and relentless, or pour like honey; in a gentle breeze it sprinkles itself over the surface, or on sultry afternoons stretches across the bay with the shallow tinfoil glitter that Ernest calls 'that shine', a sign of unsettled weather on the way.

The world from the tower turns and turns about me, and insulated by the steady hum of the intricately-balanced mechanism, I am reminded of how the light-keepers used to speak of their all-night watch from midnight until eight in the morning. 'Best time in the world,' I was told. 'You can be yourself, think your own thoughts, make a big fry-up and eat the lot. You're on your own – just you and the light.' Awake hour after quiet hour while everyone else slept, adrenalin sharpened the senses; it was vital to keep alert: lives might depend on it. All the island dwellings dark, the only signs of human life would be from towns far off on the opposite shores of Cardigan Bay and the friendly loom of distant lighthouses – South Stack, Strumble Head, the Irish rock stations if it was very clear – but in the brilliantly-lit island of the lantern room there would be only black night pressing against the windows, disturbed sometimes by a shearwater caught in the beam. A flash of white belly, perhaps the scrape of wings or claws on glass, and a dark shape falling away. On thick nights after new moon in spring and autumn there is what ornithologists call 'an attraction': migrating birds are drawn to and caught in the revolving beams, sometimes in their thousands, and the night is noisy with the flight calls of many different species. At dawn there used to be bodies piled high at the base of the tower and many more, battered or too exhausted to fly, strewn, silent, around it. Then the avian predators would arrive. For decades Trinity House worked with the RSPB and the Observatory to save lives, trying first ladder-rests on the tower, then gantry lights and now powerful lamps that attract birds away from the lighthouse to the gorse bushes instead where innumerable stunned survivors roost and recover.

Stepping outside to stand a hundred feet high on the balcony, I scan the island to note what else has changed. The boats, yes. There's the old cattle-boat, the Lleuddad, upturned now but still holding the lovely curve of its rotting planks, the same muddle of ropes, lobster-pots and buoys. There is a flash of bright bird-yellow from the big new cargo-boat by the *storws*, and so many more seal-heads bobbing in the bay – they used to keep to the west coast. The houses are painted white now, proofed against the weather. The cattle grazing the lowland fields are Welsh Blacks – Wil's herd was a mix of breeds, Hereford cross cows running with Gethin, the mottled old Shorthorn bull. The dark conifers of the plantation behind Nant are too far to see from here. If I had photographs I might recognise more that is new. But I rarely look through a camera or use binoculars: I prefer to experience through my own, imperfect senses.

Anchored in Rock

> 'Bardsey has turned its back on the world.'
>
> R.M. Lockley, *I Know an Island*, 1938

Physically, you will find the island in Cardigan Bay at latitude 52 degrees, 46 north and longitude 4 degrees 47 west. It is just over a mile and a half wide at its maximum and two and a half miles long, a strange irregular shape ending in a dribble of black rock, like a spoonful of pancake batter dropped into a hot frying pan.

If there is a single feature that gives Bardsey its character, it is the *mynydd*, the mountain. Not a mountain at all, of course, at only 548 feet, but a forbidding ridge rising steep from the sea, it is geology evident – a heap of rubble left where first the ancient sea-bed split and pulsed fire, then heaped, crumpled and folded sediments and boulders together to form what geologists call a 'melange'. Along the crest you walk on some of the oldest exposed rock in Britain, dating from the Precambrian period, six hundred million years ago. It is a jumble, streaked and squeezed together like plasticine in a giant fist, and casually discarded two miles further than the mainland. So, there is granite, flint and chert; quartz, pillow lava and huge white clusters of limestone; slate, red mudstone, strange 'eggs' of greenish dolomite and bright pebbles of jasper. Around the north-west headland lava has set into stone pillows and bubbles. A final gigantic heave oozed red-hot sludge that cooled to black basalt, fingers of softer rock stretching inland and easily sucked out by the sea to form the guts and gullies and each *ogof* (cave) of Bardsey's shoreline, the landing place at Cafn being the most notable. When ice buried even the peaks of Snowdonia, although the glaciers faltered here at the end of Llŷn they swept and shaped the hump, scouring and scratching, pushing up raised beaches on both sides of the island and plastering a layer of boulder clay over the west-facing plateau. Since the last ice-sheet melted some fifteen thousand years ago, wind and rain and rising sea have never ceased the process of erosion and re-making.

The heaped-up rocks of the mountain make Bardsey a light-filled, airy place, a haven hidden in the shelter of the sharp, steep hill. It screens the worst of the withering winds from the east and blunts the force of south-westerly gales sweeping over the patchwork of small fields crouched within their hedge-banks (I was once told there are two hundred of them, of an acre each; but I have never counted). The houses nestle in the shelter, most of them in pairs 'like mated birds', Lockley observed sweetly. They have the gorsey hill at their backs and no view of the mainland: they look out to the Irish Sea, day's end and, after sunset, glimpses of far hills, like a land of promise. All the springs rise on this gentler side, from a fold of limestone deep within the rock, an aquifer that, it is claimed, runs from St Mary's well on the mainland under the Sound to rise two miles and two hundred feet higher on Bardsey. Once, Ernest watched in awe as a water diviner directed the boat along the flow of fresh water by the energy in the metal rods he held in each hand, thrumming and dipping in response through a hundred fathoms of salt.

Small enough to see whole, big enough to hide in if you want to, the island is best seen from its backbone, where on the east side the cliff plunges straight down. Except in the first sun of a summer morning, the sea below is dark, forbidding; the rocks of the shore unforgiving, most often fringed with irritable froth or washed by a relentless, sickening surge. On shallow soil, the grass is sparse and salt-scorched and soon burns off. There is a brief flourish of foxgloves in early summer, and bracken flows and swirls like a bright green stream. There are three paths, now little more than sheep-tracks. On either side, in spring and summer, sea-birds, for this is their territory. Herring gulls and black-backed gulls loiter in casual groups above the densely-populated ledges where guillemot and razorbill throng on their stacked ledges, for they like to nest almost wing to wing. Fulmars tuck their single egg into a notch or crevice at a height from which they can sail majestically out over the waves, surfing the air currents without so much as a flap. Kittiwakes wawl and mewl and flap about. Puffins have recently colonised the softer ground between the stones of the boulder scree, ten pairs now, despite the vigilant presence of the peregrine falcon and his mate.

At the southern end the land dips and rises again in a cliff with jagged shaly edges topped by one huge crag jutting out fifty metres sheer to the sea. This is Pen Cristin, an ancient point of vantage and a lookout point where the wives waited to catch the first flash of spray as the island boat rounded the headland that hides Aberdaron. 'They're on their way back,' the keenest-eyed would report, bringing to an end an afternoon of chatter and relaxation. There was just time to scamper home and get the children tidied up and a meal on, or to stroll down to the landing place to see what the men might have brought, pounce on any news and, latterly, witness the opening of the mail bag. During the Second World War Siôn Cristin built a hut under this rock, tucked into a shallow cleft for shelter while he sent Morse code messages with his flashlight – 'speaking with the lamp' as Nell Williams called it. These days it is used in summer by dolphin-watchers for weeks on end, and unromantically nicknamed 'The Telephone Box' because it's in line with the Orange and Vodaphone masts on Rhiw mountain. For a long time, this was the only place where mobile phones would work. It was where you had to come to be in touch with the world beyond the island.

Looking Across
(from *Island of Dark Horses*)

Raven croaks and rises from the crag
where the women used to watch
the island boat, their menfolk going and returning.
Fulmars surf the air, stiff-winged. Wheeling high
towards mainland fields, young chough scream.
While we sit here the world can change.
We can blot it all out with one finger.

Round the back, the three paths narrow;
waves wink and beckon: each deck
of this tilting ship has its own dizzy catwalk,
its companion-way above the water.

I overheard an elderly woman once describing how she had tried to recreate a Polish orchard in Wales, laughing at herself a little: 'We always want the garden of our childhood, don't we, we want to lie under the first trees we knew.' And I suppose it is true: the present often doesn't live up to 'the best time' in memory. The image of Bardsey I hold in my mind is part-truth and part, I suspect, a Ladybird *Book of the Farm*, a vigorous place, with a multitude of small tasks and heavy labour at which people worked as a team and everyone had a part to play, even the cats – in every farmyard and at the lighthouse – watching for mice by the stacks. Looking after the land had its rhythm: winter was for cleaning and digging out the ponds where the cattle drank, for building up walls and opening ditches. What struck me was the directness of people, an easy confidence in themselves and their place in the way of life.

An idealised view, no doubt, but at least it was a sustainable way to live. Most produce was used on the island or sold locally; only the lobsters were sent any distance, marketed through wholesalers. Animal feed was grown on the island, and returned to the land in the form of manure that fermented in great heaps in corners of each farmyard, and sliced rich as fruit cake, not at all evil-smelling. Humans had the Victorian version of compost loos, with the waste scraped out weekly into the raised bed behind and covered with lime. After a year, it was carted out and spread on the hayfields. Apart from seaweed, no other fertiliser was ever used, and the survival of a rich variety of grasses and flowers is partly due to that. Food was rarely wasted, pigs and chickens saw to that, and surplus from the vegetable gardens was carefully preserved for the winter. There was no plastic then, only cardboard boxes and paper bags that would be burned or composted. Sugar, tea and tobacco were the main imports, packaged much the same as today, and flour in seventy-pound sacks of fine weave that would be used as the backing for rag rugs. Hessian sacks made useful capes or plucking aprons and would be re-used over and over for years. The few tins that found their way here and any bottles (jam jars would be used again) were dumped in a particular cove where strong currents quickly rusted the metal away and ground the glass back to sand. Living on an island makes people inventive: thrown on your own resources, you have to make do with what is to hand; make your own yeast or mend a harness or get the generator going. Many a cot or coffin has been knocked up out of driftwood. I remember Ernest searching the beach for a piece of cork, then trimming it to pad the clutch of his motorbike.

Donald Allchin's *Impressions of Bardsey* describes 'a place where people of our time can experience something of the rhythm, the demand and the beauty of a life not dominated by electricity and machines.' These days there is the stutter and thump of diesel engines from tractors and electricity generators, thank goodness for them, and for the clattering roar of a helicopter when you need one, though lately the snarl of a jet ski out of Abersoch, circling the island mindlessly as a wasp, has been less welcome.

The Victorian graveyard is a friendly place; the dead not pushed away from the main track of daily activity but in the middle of it. The last family in Nant used to spread their laundry over the slate tombs to dry, and the youngest daredevil children played jumping across the broken window opening twenty feet up the Abbey tower. The old Lord

Newborough lies in his lead sarcophagus under his imposing cross on a little green *maes* of farm buildings, chapel and minister's house, where the stone culvert brings fresh water gushing from the spring. When he was laid to rest, it would have bustled, with women filling buckets to rinse their washing, cattle coming to drink and a horse plodding round and round the horse-gin, turning the shaft for butter-churning or crushing oats. Now, it's a favourite picnic place for day visitors. A few ewes and lambs are always to be found calmly nibbling the lusher green that grows in the shelter of the stone walls, and the last Muscovy duck used to waddle up from the pond to sit under the white stone that remembers Lizzie Neale, the lighthouse-keeper's wife who died in childbirth aged 32. The minister's diary tells us her last words were 'O the bright beautiful home!' and Trinity House order books record bringing her sister to care for the other children.

It has remained the only permanently occupied offshore Welsh island, the only one that can still be called a home.

Island of the Imagination

'The Rome of Britain', 'the Iona of Wales', one of the three great pilgrimage places of Wales and a part of its mythology, almost a national symbol from Arthurian legend to Dafydd Iwan's *Yr Ynys,* recorded in 2006. I did not want to write about Bardsey in a misty Celtic twilight sort of way; for me, it was a place to live (to *make a living*, that lovely phrase implying hard-won satisfactions): practical, pragmatic. Myths of Merlin sleeping on that little hill with the Thirteen Treasures of Britain, or Arthur being rowed across the Sound by three Maidens in white samite – while enough to set a group of dogged Dutch systematically searching the gorse with metal detectors hidden under their waterproofs – make a soft-focus fuzz through which physical realities keep breaking. Reading the English Romantic poets over the years, I had become aware of how it was possible to use Welsh landscape to quiver the sensibilities, and I had no desire to do that. So for almost two decades I held back from publishing any of my scribbles about the island. In the end I had to write about it because it was where I was. *Island of Dark Horses* was my fourth book, a collection of poems exclusively about the island, its history and my experience of it. But I did try not to be seduced by myth – and where I construed connections not supported by historical probability, I drew attention to it as 'fictionalising'.

But all islands are fragments made significant by the sea's indifferent shifting formlessness, and meaning seems to snag and gather round them, enlarging their outlines on the horizons of the mind. Myths about them are almost universal across cultures, often as versions of the earthly paradise, for they are the perfect shape to build a dream – or a nightmare. In stories and sagas they offer opportunities, sanctuary and danger. The sea brings the adventurer. He scrambles ashore, the discoverer. And then walks up to meet whatever awaits. It might be Circe, the seductress who turns men into the beasts their appetites make of them. Perhaps there is a monster to be confronted on a hill or a treasure to be found, but there is always the danger of being trapped, stranded, castaway . . .

So Bardsey is not only a real, physical place but an island of the mind. Just to name it wakens one of two faces: Enlli, the old name gentle as a sigh, evokes a place much loved in Wales – the romantic *Island in the Current* that has become a literary commodity. Perhaps it is not a topographical reference at all but an echo of Benlli, who was variously, or both, a legendary giant or a pagan king brought down in flame by St Garmon. In the English name, the consonants *b* and *d* and the *s*, pronounced like *z* make it definite, hard-edged. And what happened in the tenth century to get people calling the place 'Bardr's isle' after an unknown Viking and *go on doing so* for a thousand years of largely Welsh occupation? It suggests an attack so horrendous or an occupation of such long standing that it was truly memorable. Welsh sources still refer to Enlli, but Giraldus Cambrensis in 1188 gives it both names, for the first time.

Its visibility inspires curiosity in the first instance. 'West of all, aloof, austere lay Bardsey Island,' mused George M.L. Davies, the famous Thirties peace worker (and uncle of my friend Gwen Robson). 'The impression of that unknown island is deepened on one's late lingering walk on headland or hill when, far away, the five fast flashes of the Bardsey lighthouse flicker across the darkness and the heart is left wistful and wondering.'

The characteristic dark hump – and the lighthouse flash – can be seen from Tre'r Ceiri high up on yr Eifl twenty-five miles north, from Dinas Dinlle near Caernarfon, from the summit of Snowdon; from Aberystwyth and all the way up the Cambrian coast to Harlech Castle. Pilgrims would have caught a glimpse of it from the little church at Mwnt.

Everyone finds it in their own way, but sometimes it hardly seems the same island. Early visitors occasionally complained of surly treatment: 'Not one friendly smile did they receive nor one civil remark addressed to them,' and even witnessed threatening behaviour when the Sabbath was broken by 'ornithological activities'. But when Davies eventually made his way to the island, at haymaking time in 1930, he was not disillusioned; not only did the landscape appear tranquil, but the residents in their 'seemly and solid' farmhouses he found hospitable and friendly: 'Their society more closely approximates that of primitive Christianity of any . . . that I have known, in the sense of that sharing community of heart and soul . . . They decide in common when it is fit to put the boat out, they suffer in common when wild weather keeps them island-bound for a month or six weeks; they share supplies when food runs short.' He saw few reminders of the most famous sanctuary of what he called the Cambro-British Church: 'Nothing remains but the whitened bones that appear with every spring ploughing, the rough crosses on stones in the farm buildings, the gravestones underfoot in the open roadway . . .' On the summit, his rapture could only be conveyed by a quotation from the mystical poet Traherne: 'The skies were mine and so were the sun and moon and stars and all the world and I the only spectator and enjoyer of it.'

His second crossing a couple of days before Christmas in the same year was very different. 'The Sound was ominous in the darkness with the swirl of great waters against black rocks towering above. The familiar cove was alternately pitch dark and brilliantly lit by the flashes from the lighthouse. The heavy boat could not reach the ship's cradle on the slip and so be hauled to safety. I scrambled over the slippery seaweed and rocks ashore, leaving the men waist-deep in water . . .' He stumbled up the lane to Cristin, where the men returned after three hours working and waiting to haul the *cwch mawr* into safety. 'If only we had an engine,' he was told, 'it would save us all this wetting and waiting for tides.'

Even these days (perhaps especially now we have TravelMadeEasy.com and its ilk) just getting there is still unexpectedly difficult – booking a boat, clambering into it, crossing an alien element in increasingly uncertain weather – so that when we land it is with some of the euphoria of adventurers. We have reached a place apart. It might be a threshold; it is encircled, easily defended, a sanctuary.

A precious, unsullied place of safety at the end of life is how medieval Welsh literature presents it. To poets and the princes they wrote for, it represented an ancient holiness, where, if anywhere, the soul could be redeemed by repentance so that it might not be lost in eternal darkness but gathered in to the *henllain*, the original or mother-hive, in Einion ap Gwalchmai's phrase. This is the sense in Meilyr's famous 'death-bed' poem with its lovely, disarming familiarity and faith in a personal saviour: 'Christ of the foretold cross, who knows me, he'll save me . . .' My translation cannot recreate the power of alliteration and internal rhyme of the original which still resonates across more than eight centuries:

> *am ei mynwent, mynwes heli*
> *Ynys Fair firain, ynys glân y glein*
> *Gwrthrych dadwyrain; ys cain yndi.*
> *Crist croes ddarogan, a'm gûyr a'm gwarchan*
> *Rhag uffern affan, wahan westi.*
> *Creawdwr a'm crewys a'm cynnwys i*
> *Ymhlith plwyf gwirin gwerin Enlli.*

'*Plwyf*' is the word in modern Welsh, used on Council Tax bills for where we live, the parish, and '*gwerin*' means the ordinary people. There is a democracy of salvation suggested: it is not only for monks and the high-born, but for all, a sort of family in the place of the resurrection.

from Death-bed Lament (*Marw-ysgafn*)

Many a time I won gold, and silk garments
from mortal princes as reward for my praise;
but in place of the muse, a power more mighty
weakens my tongue towards poorness and silence.

I – Meilyr the poet – am now pilgrim to Peter
the guard at the gate who weighs everyone's worth.
When it is time for us all in the grave
to be roused, O then may he raise me!
Awaiting that call, let me lie quiet
in the cloister cleansed by the flood-tide.
Undying the fame of that hermitage,
its graves a sweet refuge in a bosom of salt.

Radiant Mary's island, pure-shining,
where the path of resurrection's bright
and Christ of the foretold cross who knows me
will save me from loss in hell's lonely lodging.
The creator who made me, he will hold and enfold me
amongst the pure folk in the parish of Enlli.

Meilyr ap Brydydd (1100–1137), trans. CE

However close to heaven it may seem to some people, the attempt to tag the island as Avalon seems an adornment too far. In *Journey to Avalon: Final Discovery of King Arthur*, 1993, Chris Barber and David Pykitt based their entire argument on a particular reading of a family tree for one of many Arthurs, along with a few place-names interpreted without much knowledge of Welsh. I do not recognize the island they describe, with Morgan Le Fay growing apples in a great glass-house built by Merlin, and am amused by the way we pick and mix from the wealth of stories at our disposal. Bardsey is fertile ground for legend, but it is too real for Camelot, too anchored in rock and full of squelch and slither and the stench of rotting seaweed.

Mythologizing can create its own backlash, as in Harri Webb's waspish poem 'Enlli':

> No, I've never been there, with luck never shall,
> Would be bored stiff in five minutes. All islands
> Of this size are horribly alike, fit only
> For sheep, saints and lighthousekeepers . . .
> Almost, but not quite, nowhere.

'Trying to spell out the history of the island,' Mary Chitty wrote, 'is like watching the island itself from the headland. Sometimes the outline is clear and hard, its detail visible; more often, in shifting gleaming light and shadows it seems to dissolve and float away. Sometimes it disappears altogether in fog. Then only the mountain saying amen to the lighthouse tells us that Bardsey is still there.'

Subtle Additions: interpretations by artists

'I love the way nothing is wasted on that island.'

Trudi Entwistle

Brenda Chamberlain found Bardsey 'a sanctuary and a prison', though when she first arrived in 1946 it was only the first she saw. A year later, she and Jean van de Bijl took the tenancy of Carreg and farmed it for six years. Brenda started to paint again, finding new subjects and a style of her own after a period of artistic bleakness. She painted life on the island: fishermen, horses, children, and boats. Gauguin's influence can be seen in the bold colours, patterned backgrounds, the strong faces and boats more elegant and high-prowed than her subjects. In 1950 she had her first single show at the Gimpel Fils Gallery in London; the following year *Girl with a Siamese Cat* (Nellie's daughter Jane the model), won a Gold Medal at the National Eisteddfod and so, in 1952, did *The Cristin Children.*

From 1951 onwards Brenda spent most winters in Germany or the south of France and her work on the island changed. Lyrical paintings like *Man with a John Dory* gave way to more abstract and atmospheric depictions of the relationship between rock and the human body, with a recurring theme of metamorphosis (*Man Rock*). Hard line-drawings turn into obsessive patterning like totems, a mosaic of eyes; fish – lustrous, once, supple with life – lie dull-eyed, gaping. The sea – often red as a wound – is glimpsed only through apertures and gashes. In 1958 *The Green Heart*, a book of poems, was published, and in 1962, *Tide-race*. By this time Brenda had left Bardsey for good. She died in Bangor in 1971 aged 59.

Kim Atkinson makes strong, bold oil paintings and woodcuts of the natural world. Lessons with her mother at the kitchen table in Tŷ Nesaf started her off: 'Both my parents had a strong interest in the environment. My mother did lovely, simple line-drawings.' Despite always being busy – as I remembered, washing clothes, feeding the pigs, boiling up dyes for the wool she spun – she taught the children in an inspired and original way, through their love of being outdoors. 'We'd go for a walk, then come back and tell Mum what we wanted to say. She'd write it down for us to copy in our Nature diaries, and then we did a drawing or a painting.' Though the family left when she was seven, Kim came back to the island for working holidays and, after her MA from the Royal Academy, 'deliberately, to learn to draw birds, get the essence of them, in context – not in the zoo'. Long days sketching and observing, and nights in a sleeping bag on the mountain, gave her an unerring eye for the stance and body language of birds in their groupings. She stayed until 1995 and now lives as near as possible, in

Uwchmynydd, with her husband Gwydion and eight-year-old son Robat. Her aim is still to show animals and landscape as they are, but she has also produced a series of striking woodcuts of life on Bardsey. Her success is considerable, and growing, her latest venture being intensely-lit paintings from drawings she made underwater, wearing diving gear.

In 1999 Cywaith Cymru (Artworks Wales) established a Millennium programme of residencies for artists on the island, with the Bardsey Island Trust providing accommodation. The first was Trudi Entwistle, a landscape artist from Leeds keen to hear island stories and to increase her knowledge of Welsh, her grandmother's language. Daily through August we encountered her *Subtle Additions* as she called her project, which she explained as, 'things nearly not there that make you see the place differently'. Crescents of tawny reeds were woven into the grass beside the main track; a row of limpets like sightless eyes stared from the tide-line; flotsam rope washed up on the shore was tweaked into configurations of the tide; sinuous lines of stones or slate or driftwood – what she called shadow captures – crawled across quiet coves. She worked mostly on the edge of the island, between rock and sea. 'This is where the drama was, the most transient and changing place.' In a shadowed gully sticks of bleached driftwood became a ladder or a walkway. Next day, arranged in spirals they glinted white as whale teeth and, as the light changed, turned into fossil shapes. Three or four children came to see what I was looking at, and ran their spades along the swirls as though it was a giant xylophone. After a month, the big autumn tide swept all the pieces into a neat stack to be discovered and used as kindling. 'That's what's exciting,' Trudi said. 'It's so ephemeral: everything I make is going to be absorbed back into the earth or scattered by the wind and waves.' From the start she was sensitive to the feelings of people living on the island: 'It was their place and I was altering their environment. I enjoyed talking to the longer-term residents, whether it was a farmer, birdwatcher or fisherman, I found there was illuminating comment from each . . . The island relies on communication between its inhabitants, as their work is so interconnected. I am glad I was part of it even for so short a time.'

Her most enduring installation was a sort of orrery, an ordered spiral of old aluminium buoys suspended in the boathouse, floating in air rather than water. Even that, though, was dismantled and tidied away. 'Everything I found will be used again.'

For the second residency Ben Stammers, a local painter and photographer, was chosen to work with the thousand or so Gwynedd children then in their final year of primary school, who were invited to visit Bardsey as its Millennium Project. It also included a six-week residency for six writers, three English and three Welsh, with the help of the Poetry Society and the Welsh Arts Council. Working with up to a hundred children a day was exhausting, but Ben still managed to produce stunning images from digitally-enhanced and combined photographs, and a couple of portraits of island residents.

Claire Barber, a textile artist from Southampton, works by sensing the emotions of a place and using local materials to create appropriate images; in Bratislava, she photographed a shower of red feathers from a tower window; in Bosnia, scattered coins frozen in the lake represented the wishes of children she had worked with; in Australia's 'Cinderella state' she made dresses fragile and bright as butterflies and wore a golden one herself in the old gold-fields of Kalgoorlie. Travelling with nomadic people in Mongolia, she had taken part in making felt for a *ger*, a wedding gift from the community for a young couple. In 2001, she was Bardsey Artist in Residence.

'The island was strikingly beautiful, but almost eerily quiet,' she remembers. (All the sheep had been taken to the mainland because of a change in management.) 'There was fleece caught on bushes but no movement or calls. Opposite the Abbey ruins was the cowshed where I was to live and work for the next six weeks. I swung open the huge gate door. It was cold and dark inside. Beneath my feet was a cobbled floor below which were the bones of all the saints . . . I was unsure how I should live and work in this place. In fact I wasn't sure if I even wanted to touch it.' *Stepping Lightly* became her theme.

'The first thing I unpacked was a pair of felt slippers I had made in Mongolia, a pair of carders and packets of tea for anyone I might meet. Lois, a child who spent each summer on the island, talked of her sadness at the departure of the sheep – which may have been descended from those brought here by the monks. She told me of the swing there used to be in this barn, and that gave me the idea for moving around my home without treading on the floor. The island seemed to me ancient and enduring but also fragile. I wanted to explore but not to disturb anything. I found my days were shaped by the day-to-day processes of collecting water, cooking, washing in the courtyard. I felt myself changing, becoming aware of things I'd taken for granted.'

She began gathering wool, and made felt boots for Lois. By the time she had twelve swings in her barn more and more children arrived on her doorstep to play on them, and soon she had them all carding bits of fleece and making it into felt slippers. Moulded directly on to each child's foot, they were a perfect fit and unique memento of that place and time, and I know of several pairs, long outgrown, that are treasured still.

'I shall never forget Bardsey's beautiful night skies and shooting stars. So I thought, the islanders needed a warm, water-resistant cloak to wear while watching the stars.' Felt seemed appropriate, and the mammoth task of carding and compressing the wool took weeks, even though Claire was helped by nearly everyone on the island. Once the wool was incorporated into a soggy mass, it was compressed by trampling. We all stamped and danced on it – to music from Claire's radio – six or seven of us at a time. 'A particular sequence of steps ensured even and consistent felting and soon felt dances evolved.' It brought everyone together and was fun, as well as resulting in a large square that Claire cut and dried in the sun. She added felt buttons, dyed with blackberry juice, and invited people to try it. It is kept in the school, hanging by the fireplace, and is used.

Susan Adams called her residency *Waiting for Something.* She explained: 'Bardsey has been known for centuries as a waiting place between life and death. Just to get there was special. And yes, as your boat is buffeted around by the Sound's conflicting currents midway between the tip of the Llŷn peninsula and the island, fear jostling with elation spreads all over you. Once you have rounded the mountain you no longer see the mainland, you have passed into another world.

'My ideas were continually being blown apart by my new-found life-in-the-present. The island too, was very difficult to pin down; despite its sometimes violent history it could possess an almost veil-like quality, between this world and somewhere else. In the paintings the island becomes transparent and the colours washed-out, whereas the people are very solid and vibrant. I thought I was going to be solitary, but it was one of the most social environments I've ever worked in.'

She was fascinated by the idea of an island hermit, and asked about Sister Helen Mary and the loft where she had lived. In her report for the Arts Council she described a 'performance' piece: 'In later years when isolation had got the better of her, the Sister would strictly adhere to the directions given by God as to what she must have for dinner, or where to cut gorse that day. My interest in the arbitrary nature of what can be read as a "Sign" suggested a video/action piece that I carried out in the last week. In one of the outhouses still sits her home-made cart. I borrowed it and filled it with pebbles with answers written on the reverse side, and dressed up as St Isiona I went around the island offering people to select an answer to their question.'

Each year, other artists come to stay. Philip Brennan, a painter and singer from County Clare, is one who is drawn back again and again. 'You have nowhere else to go, no worldly distraction, no excuse not to paint. The day's concerns are weather, tide, light and the island's small comings and goings.' He's particularly interested in trying to capture the sea as its roughest, and one year he painted Maen Du through no fewer than three gales.

And there is Carole Shearman, who works across several media – oil, watercolour, charcoal, ink for print-making, clay, wool – and with true humility calls herself a *craftsperson*. Since 2006 she has come for the whole season, four months or more, to live in Nant loft and stable. Her kitchen is her studio and workplace. On any given day you will find small groups of visitors interpreting their experience of the island with her help, making pots or clay birds she will fire before they leave, carding wool to make rugs and wall-hangings or painting. For day visitors, too, her door is always open and her own work, even her wonderfully expressive journals, available to see.

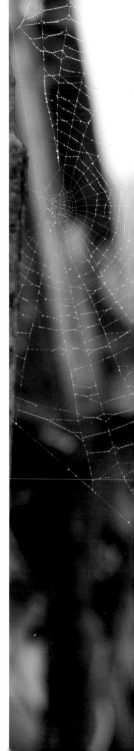

Inheritors

> Who possesses this landscape?
> The man who bought it or
> we who are possessed by it?
>
> Norman MacCaig

If a place is regarded as remote, abandoned, lonely, its people will be seen as castaways or primitives, recently as drop-outs; at best, oddities. The popular view of Bardsey is romantically empty, a Crusoe place: the television crews ask us to get off the track or leave the beach while they're filming, or cut shots that include people other than the wildlife presenter or solitary farmer.

Sometimes there is a mixture of envy and resentment in the comments of summer visitors – 'Oh, you are so *lucky*' – though after a few days of stormy weather in August, a sort of mental shudder becomes apparent: 'What is it like in the winter?' as they imagine creeping out to the privy, surviving dark days without electricity or the distractions of company, parties, shopping. Then, inhabitants seem engaged in a heroic struggle. As though the island were just a backdrop to a drama of survival.

It is true that one can feel besieged by weather, when the full force of a severe gale sucks and tugs at the roof. Yes, the island can be bleak but it is not barren: for most of human history it has been seen as a rich place, with seas and shore swarming with life, albeit of the sort we scorn to consider as food these days. True, the one fact of being on an island means you cannot leave just when you want, but isolation is another matter. One of the hermit nuns used to say she would be far more alone in a city flat, for it is impossible to be ignored in a small community.

The lives of the monks would have been intertwined with the colours and rhythms of the world about them; Celtic Christianity saw creatures, men and women, angels and the natural world as intricately linked features of Creation – one whole. They read the psalms and said their prayers according to the changing light and day-length, the services of the hours beginning with Lauds at dawn, and Vespers after sunset. They lived in the sound of the wind and the waves, worked with the tides gathering shell-fish and tending nets and stone fish-traps. Celtic monks in Ireland have left eloquent if brief testimonies to a fulfilling relationship with the earth and a sense of wonder and delight in it (perhaps the first written evidence of a sense of beauty in nature). This wasn't pantheistic: birdsong in April or patterns of light on the sea raised awareness and directed gratitude and delight to their creator.

> *His is the earth to his will; it is he who moves the sea; both hath he endowed, the one with plants, the other with sea-creatures. He is the most generous: he is a hospitaller in possessions; his is every flock, his the wild beasts and the tame.*

There is no possessiveness in this, no urge to own or control. It's more a hunter-gatherer sense of abundance than a farmer's desire to exploit the potential of landscape. Creatures are respected for their own sake; given the space to be themselves within the pattern of the seasons. Elsewhere in Europe from the early eighth century, the sense of man as a being divided between the angelic and the bestial, ever susceptible to temptation, led to the rejection of Nature's appeal to the senses. It was a sort of seduction to be vigorously repudiated, even destroyed. Unlike the creation-centred prayers of the Celtic monks such as Patrick and Dewi, the emphasis was on redemption and inherited sin.

This conflict, or its manifestations, still fascinates. Susan Adams, who spent six weeks on the island as an Artist in Residence seemed obsessed by the mutilations and humiliations of the flesh that she associated with sainthood. She took photographs of the residents and then painted us 'as saints waiting for the touch of something Other'. The first portrayals were of self-torturing figures – a naked Stylite, a maiden chained on the rocks – though these were adapted for the final collection. Others – perhaps potentially more damaging because we couldn't laugh at them – implied disturbing psychological insights. 'Everyone seemed unusual in some way, friendly and open with their thoughts,' the artist reported, almost echoing George Davies' remarks fifty years earlier: 'The welcome at the farm is so naïve, the hospitality so natural, the talk so frank and intimate.' With no idea of her project, we assumed it was the island, not us, that was of interest. We became 'material' for her, and the same was true of the young writer Fflur Dafydd who produced what she called a 'novel' based on anecdotes and actions she observed within the island community during her short stay. In this respect, she was following Brenda Chamberlain, who was unable to resist the temptation to turn some of her island neighbours into grim caricatures; but at least Chamberlain had the respect to dedicate *Tide-race* to them, and to change their names more subtly. To substitute *Twm* for Tom, *Alys* for Alice, *Dic* for Mick as Fflur Dafydd did in *Atyniad* is to thumb the nose at conventions of fictional characters. Perhaps people who live on an island, outlandish, against the norm, have no right to resent being appropriated; as though in these days of reality TV shows and the great democracy of celebrity, we should welcome exposure. In a tourist economy, must islanders be just props in the landscape like those picturesque 'hermits' engaged by eighteenth-century landowners to furnish grottoes on their estates? As a family we were glad to return to the anonymity of Uwchmynydd that year.

One of the important dynamics of a community in a small place has to be respect for privacy. Living in Llŷn I had been struck by this – when I came to read a Robert Frost poem that begins 'Good neighbours need good fences', I understood exactly why. In a small place it only needs one discordant note, one person who doesn't know or accept the common code of shared values, and things are out of tune. That is especially important when people are interdependent, and working together is essential. Until the arrival of tractors, the first in about 1956, (Twm Nant did have a Fordson earlier but it was never shared), it was impossible to pull up or launch the boat without your neighbours' assistance: *Five to launch, four to row, and one to steer* went the saying. Moving heavy objects – a water tank, say – would be a team effort, as was driving the sheep off the mountain and sorting them into their separate flocks.

Bardsey people were financially better off than their equivalents on the mainland. 'If you stay twenty years, you leave a rich man,' Siôn Cristin used to say. Well, they had the sea to farm as well as the land – herring, then oyster, then lobsters and crabs. And the

land was fertile and early: crops grew well, nourished by a rich mixture of animal dung and seaweed. Barley was grown, and sold as seed-corn, free from diseases, a high-value crop it was worth taking to Liverpool. All it cost was hard labour. And there was cash coming in, with not much to spend it on.

There's testimony to relative wealth (or low expectations) in the number of people listed as 'servants' on the census returns, at least two for every house – a young man for farm work, and a girl to help in the house. It is easy for us to underestimate the amount of labour required even on a small holding of twenty acres or so before mechanisation, as Dr Arnold does in *Enlli* when he suggests that so many female farm servants implies that they were 'effectively prostitutes' (*puteiniaid*) for unmarried sons. As an urban academic (and a man) perhaps we should not expect him to realise that the housewife's duties would include responsibility for all the dairy work and looking after poultry, pigs and other yard animals, as well as taking care of the kitchen garden. Field crops were men's responsibility: maincrop potatoes, turnips, carrots and, in the nineteenth century, patches of what the old people called *pupus* or 'small grey peas', vetches that were valuable as cattle feed. In times of hardship, the islanders even ate the tubers, dried or roasted. But everything else, all the greens and fruit for puddings and preserves, the herbs to make salted or smoked meat more palatable in winter and any more tender vegetables like broad beans or early potatoes would be grown in the walled gardens close to the house, and qualified as women's work.

In addition, it was common for island women to spend some time on the mainland with mothers or sisters, especially during confinements. The work still needed to be done. If they had no daughters old enough, a 'maid' was almost essential, and they were often relatives: a sort of 'adolescent-swap' was traditional, and gave each youngster a taste of somewhere different and the chance to learn work-skills under the discipline of someone not too close. After the island school closed when Ernest was seven, Nellie and her daughter alternated weeks staying on the mainland with him – which Jane, then in her early twenties, relished.

Because they are seen as closed communities, it is not uncommon for islands to be seized on for the study of cultural process. But the Bardsey population saw themselves as an extension of the mainland community, and crossed regularly, twice a week if they could, to Aberdaron; the men kept spare clothes in the village, where sisters and daughters had found husbands, and if they couldn't get home, there were informal arrangements for earning board and lodging at several farms along the coast. So any study of their culture must be seen in context with that of the village, where even now surnames are not much used in day-to-day affairs – people are identified by a patronymic and place of birth ('Twm Nant's son', for example.) Studying Bardsey census records of a hundred and fifty years ago, an outsider might well find it 'difficult to establish the actual extent of illegitimacy and incest' but takes it for granted because 'the interchange of surnames . . . leads to the strong suspicion that many of the families were interrelated in other ways . . .' (*Enlli*.)

The 'suspicion' expressed seems to fit the tendency to both romanticise and belittle the islanders, rather than see them as decent, ordinary human beings. Roy Campbell, the South African poet, 'escaped' to a rural idyll in Rhiw in the Twenties, and left an account of the people of Bardsey in his autobiography:

> I wrote letters for the peasants and became King Love's chief adviser concerning his home policy: and cheating the tax-collector. Love was about eighty then. He could pick up a sack of flour with one hand and lay it over his shoulder as if it were a feather. I heard from him, rather through him (for he couldn't write) several times since, in Africa: until I saw the announcement of his sudden death, and saw that the islanders had left; which I think is silly of them. Few of them could speak a word of English . . .

Even the parts of his account that are not fictional – there is no evidence that Campbell ever visited Bardsey – are unreliable. In the 1901 census only eleven people, the oldest, were listed as speaking only Welsh; for generations the island children had gone to school with those from the lighthouse, and in a letter to Lord Newborough the minister

149

pointed out the extra work involved in preaching in English 'for the sake of the lighthouse'. Campbell's attempt to make the islandmen exotic – 'most wore earrings and beards' – was disputed by Nel Carreg, who lived on the island at that time. Only one of the men ever wore an ear-ring, and that because he was hard of hearing and had been told it might help!

The tendency persists. Brenda Chamberlain probably continued it, needing colourful characters for *Tide-race*. A more recent newspaper article entitled *Marooned on Bardsey at Whitsuntide* implied surprise that the farmer's wife 'conversed amiably and intelligently in a sensitive clear speech which seemed completely uninfluenced by modernity. One was strongly reminded of those modest heroines depicted in pioneering films'. Even Jim Perrin in his essay 'Island Artist', can't resist romanticising his subject: 'Kim speaks in the distant, surprised pitch of one grown away from the habits of conversation.'

I recall Mary Chitty, the Bardsey historian, saying, 'Everyone is very much himself there, for good or bad,' and it is true that the island has grown its own tyrants and scapegoats, but it is generally the outsiders drawn to the place who are unconventional or in turmoil, and they who feel isolated. Ernest – and Kim, who also grew up in the first place she remembered – cannot really describe their childhood as different from that of anyone else: it just was. I imagine that the *hen bobl*, the 'old people', the 'Bardseys' or indigenous islanders, would have taken the details of their lives for granted in the same way. They had a relationship to the island similar to that of sheep 'hefted' to their own ground. It was simply a small world that they were part of, where they belonged.

> *those men*
> *standing there like everybody's ancestors*
> *fall into the texts of specialists*
>
> Douglas Dunn, *St Kilda's Parliament*

Eligugs and Others

'Bardsey should be left for the birds'

John Barnie

In the seventeenth century, John Ray – who visited Bardsey in 1662 – thought of his interest in birds and animals as worship, studying the Creation, and there is something religious about the dedication of scientists. I have to admit the fascination of talking to the experts staying at the Observatory; I learn something amazing every time, such as the numbers of daddy-long-leg species, the habits of wood-mice or how all cuckoo wrasse are female until the need arises for some of them to change sex. Perhaps lichenologists qualify as the Calvinistic Methodists of Natural History for their intensity of focus.

Lichens are such strange organisms, a partnership between fungus, related to truffles or morels and green algae, the sort of thing you see in summer ponds. And Bardsey – perhaps because of its variety of rocks as well as its clean air – is particularly rich in species, 430 at the last count, with 84 'of national importance'. Most evident is the radiant yellow *Xanthoria* that clothes the roof of the boathouse, cleverly matched by the landing craft *Maria Stella*. The grey-green spiky stuff, like living pumice, that covers rocks by the sea is *Ramalina*, which thrives on salt winds. Tree lungwort (*Lobaria Pulmonaria*) is one of the few that have a common name, because of its medicinal usage through the ages; it still appears in modern herbals.

Yes, I think I could fall in love with lichen too, if it weren't for all the other things to intrigue the mind and gladden the heart. Last year I sat down to make a list of reasons why Bardsey is a National Nature Reserve and Site of Special Scientific Interest. I got to twenty-three general categories – rare plants, dolphins and porpoises, butterflies, slugs, marine life and so on – before I gave up and went out for a walk. The more you look, the more you find. There's a wood-mouse drowned in a bucket. You take it up to the Observatory for identification and learn that, free of competition, the wood-mice here grow unusually large; it's called gigantism. An eel slithers from the well, perhaps starting its journey back across the Atlantic; tiny blue stars of spring squill and thrift, *clustog Fair*

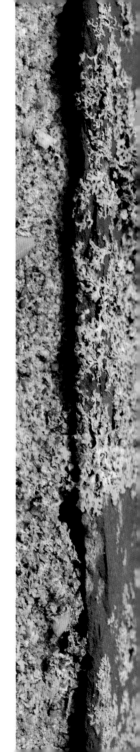

or Mary's pillow spread across the Narrows; peregrines scream on the crags behind the house, inciting their young out of the nest. *Fly! Fly! Air's what you're meant for!* and demonstrating with amazing displays of steep climbs and zooms. Marsh marigolds and mushrooms stroke soft as calf-skin, warm and slightly damp. And seal song permeates not only your waking hours but also your dreams.

They slouch and lounge, the seal congregations at their singing, nonchalant, blubbery sacks or roll sinuously, turning smooth bellies to the sun, creamy fawn or mottled grey.

Even after a hundred years, it's said, a sealskin will bristle in damp weather, as if remembering the sea. Their flippers are like human hands, five fingers webbed with skin, and used as delicately as hands to scratch a belly or waft a fly from a nose. They will close a fist and scratch the back of it with five long black nails or tickle a palm. They gaze unblinking with deep-set, divers' eyes. They are not pretty, with their heavy Neanderthal skulls, but there have always been legends that they can come ashore in human form. In the Thirties, a cousin of Lord Newborough, Captain Dick Kneeshaw of the Royal Welsh Fusiliers, used to stay in Plas Bach to shoot seal for their skins. Gwyndon Williams of Nant told me of the thrill of stalking along the west coast with him until his father refused to let him go. The Captain was sufficiently enthusiastic to write and publish an illustrated guide to harpooning, *Seal-hunting along the North Wales Coast*. Despite the competition for fish, the older islanders were not easy with the idea of slaughtering the creatures – although fifty years earlier, glee is evident in the description in *Tomos o Enlli* of catching a fine bull in Ogof Morlo, that was for meat and oil.

Seals wail and moan like discontented souls. They could well embody the souls of drowned fishermen, for like them, at sea they seem always looking to the land, but once there, they yearn to be out again. And a hungry seal pup sounds exactly like a human baby. One autumn I began a story of a childless woman driven wild by the needy cries, but I discovered Brenda Chamberlain was before me:

> I dreamed that once I was a lonely woman living on a desert beach, without husband, without children, and if in the spring I was crowned it was with sea-

tangle of my own weaving. One day, so great was my desire to be a mother that I stole a baby seal, silken-haired and innocent from a rock spray blew over. What a temper it had! It bit and scratched and tore its own face furiously when it could not get at mine. It screamed with the voice of any human child. The bereft cow roared and came up from the surf to beat my doors and windows with her flippers. She blew like a whale through the keyhole; she moaned and whimpered for her little bull. At last she was forced by lack of success to go back to the cold wastes of the sea and I was left in peace. My adopted child grew listless, the fight went out of it, and at last it pined away, dwindling inside its long fur. It died; then, I went to live far away from the seals' breeding ground.

O seal cow in the cavern! Your mournful eyes . . .

(from *Tide-race*)

Seal pups are born in autumn. The seal cows come ashore to feed the pups three or four times a day. Their milk is rich, very high in butterfat, so the pups triple their weight in the first three weeks of life, filling out their loose white coats. They can be watched sleeping among the rocks in sheltered coves. Some mothers are most attentive, watching offshore, and even calling bigger pups down to the water. When they venture in, or get washed out by a big wave, they have no problems swimming, though their coats don't seem to be fully waterproof and they show signs of feeling the cold. As soon as the pups moult their white fluff, the mothers lose interest: they are old enough to fend for themselves. The cow – who will have mated three days after giving birth – abandons her pup and joins the roistering, groaning, farting throng on the rocks in the Honllwyn. The extremely fat youngster stays on the beach for another week or ten days, sleeping most of the day or playing by itself in rock-pools or with pebbles, until hunger calls it to the sea.

The seabirds' clamour begins as soon as it starts to get light. What Harri Webb called (with some irritation) 'the gulls' gymanfa, the endless eisteddfod of eligugs' is best appreciated from a boat 'round the back'. The three narrow paths are rarely walked now so they have become sheep-tracks, treacherous as catwalks on a vertiginous tilting

deck. Here in 1891 a lighthouse-keeper, out shooting rabbits, fell to his death. There are no records of any islanders lost. Not that they didn't go there: Nellie thought nothing of tripping along the bottom path to look out for late lambs or a straying dog. In fifty years, there have been a couple of incidents of Observatory volunteers having falls and having to be lifted off to hospital by an RAF helicopter.

From the safer vantage-point of a boat the sharp contours glide easily by, their tenants exposed. First, on Pen Cristin, are the crowded ledges of the onomatopoeically nicknamed guillemots (eligugs) and razorbills with their oddly shaped eggs; then the shrieking kittiwake colony and scatters of squabbling fulmar. Look close and there might be a few puffins – ten pairs bred here last year – but above, buzzard and black-backed gull circle. Among the big fallen boulders of Briw Gerrig shags sulk in their slum tenements and above Ogof Morlas ravens patrol the gull colony on the corner. There may be chough feeding on the grassy slopes, strutting about with a confident air and a keen eye. The wildest of the crow family, they need sheep to graze closely so they can get at the little insects they like. In the air they are bow-shaped, and they flash their wings as they shriek, delirious with excitement.

The best time for birds – perhaps the best time on the island – is the end of summer into autumn. For migrants in their thousands Bardsey is still a sanctuary, a place to rest and feed; a landmark they will recognise on their ancestral routes, and at night a beacon in the shape of the lighthouse. To stand on the southern tip of the island under big flocks of purposeful curlew or thousands of thrushes stirs the blood, but many birds make solitary journeys, and these are the most moving. Look out from anywhere at dusk and there will be small groups of waders dwarfed by the swell, making their way over deep water, setting off on their night journey in the last light of the sky; or a single cormorant against the darkening sea.

Migration is an ongoing wonder. How can such birds – some tiny, an eighth of an ounce, like a goldcrest, say, so fragile you hardly feel it on your palm – make such epic journeys, mostly at night to be safer? I have stood by the lighthouse wall watching the birds circling it, mesmerised and held in the travelling beam, and then spotted an

154

opportunist owl perched nearby, watching for one to break away or fall to the ground. Ornithologists will explain how every bird is acutely attuned to the time of year and to diurnal rhythms, and migrating species – as I understand it – have internal compasses. That tiny goldcrest has three tiny magnetite crystals embedded in its head, and navigates by the sun and stars as well.

As you listen to enthusiasts, windows open and go on opening into intricate patterns of animal life. The kestrel, for example, can see into the ultra-violet, so when it hovers, scanning, it is reading neon-bright yellow spots of voles' urine between the gorse bushes, signposting burrows where the tiny mammals are cowering, waiting for a chance to make a run for it.

For a dozen years a kestrel made its roost in the ruined Abbey. We startled each other once: I was sheltering from rain, huddled on the little driftwood bench and reflecting how wind and weather had worn the shape of the entrance and window-holes into ragged echoes of the caves on the west coast, sea-mouths in sandstone, when it swooped in and instantly out again in a scurry of disturbed air. Telling the Obs. warden, I was astonished to hear that the little pile of pellets beside the makeshift altar had been sifted to reveal the remains of over a hundred of my favourite small birds: wrens, robins and goldcrests.

Of all the encounters on the island, I never fail to thrill to the shearwaters' arcing cries as they try to come to earth safely and complete the circle. It seems to me energy incarnate. The darker the night, the more tumultuous their cries. Norse sagas from the tenth century that describe 'night ravens' swooping in noisy attack as bad omens before battles must refer to shearwaters. I wonder if they ever saved the monks of Bardsey from slavery or slaughter. The most up-to-date reference is probably from Richard Dawkins's book *The God Delusion*. He is arguing the unreliability of personal experience as proof of faith:

One of the cleverer and more mature of my undergraduate contemporaries, who was deeply religious, went camping in the Scottish isles. In the middle of the night

he and his girlfriend were woken in their tent by the voice of the devil, Satan himself; there could be no possible doubt: the voice was in every sense diabolical. My friend would never forget this horrifying experience, and it was one of the factors that later drove him to be ordained. My youthful self was impressed by this story, and recounted it to a gathering of zoologists relaxing in the Rose and Crown Inn, Oxford. Two of them happened to be experienced ornithologists, and they roared with laughter. 'Manx Shearwater!' they shouted in delighted chorus. One of them added that the diabolical shrieks and cackles of this species have earned it, in various parts of the world and various languages, the local nickname 'Devil Bird'.

At sea, the shearwater looks holy, a flying cross, with wings held stiffly at right angles to the body, and its plumage is monastic as well: it flicks from black to white underside as it travels low over the waves. I like to go out in the boat on summer evenings to see them 'rafting', gathered on the sea in their thousands, waiting for thick night. There will be long ragged shadows lying on the water, rising from time to time to wheel round before settling again in a silently-bobbing sombre quilt. They do not seem perturbed by our presence or the boat riding quietly alongside until chill shadows drive us back to our own nests before dark.

They have long narrow wings and webbed feet, set far back on the body, so while they are perfectly adapted to two elements, on land they can only blunder and shuffle, which is why they are so vulnerable. As a species, they are amazingly long-lived, as the famous one ringed here in 1957 and again by Steve in 2004 and 2005 testifies. *World's Oldest Bird*, trumpeted the headlines, calculating that she – for of course the female is always the tougher – must have flown over five million miles during her life. The bond with her mate, if he has survived, will be renewed when they meet each year in March to clean out their burrows. After mating, the female flies back to the Bay of Biscay to feed on sardines while the single large egg grows inside her. The male stays nearby, visiting the burrow each night to ensure that no other bird takes it over. Once his mate has laid the egg, usually in mid-May, he takes the first incubation stint. After that the pair take it in turns, a few days at a time. It will be over seven weeks before it hatches, and the chick will need a further ten before it can leave the underground nest, the longest of any British bird.

Both parents feed it generously and it grows into a fat ball of grey fluff. In September the adults leave and the chicks are left alone. It is at this time that we come across them standing outside their burrows like old men staring up at the sky. All summer the ringers have been busy trying to catch and record as many as possible. Ringing shearwaters never happens on a nice, dry night; it is always thick dark, usually in the small hours, often raining and commonly in dense fog. It involves plodding or scrambling over rough terrain among a straggle of Observatory staff and visitors. Wading through wet bracken in bobbing circles of torchlight, the only sounds are rustling waterproofs and ragged breath. There is no sign of shearwaters, or any other form of life; they've all got more sense than to be out on a night like this. Then, the warden kneels and shoves his arm into a hole in the bank. It disappears to well above the elbow. Once, this is how the birds were harvested on islands less productive than this one, to be eaten both fresh and pickled. Long ago, I've read, the oil from their bodies was used for preventing armour from rusting and as lamp fuel.

To watch and wonder is enough. Steve exclaims as his hand is met by a sharp hooked beak, and again, swallowing expletives as he draws out a slim black adult bird that is very annoyed. Someone shines a torch. 'It's got a ring,' Steve reports. 'Number FC eight-eight-four-twenty. Got that down?'

Bird FC88420 is very vocal, and energetic, even in Steve's experienced hands, and nobody seems particularly keen to take him while the burrow is explored further. But there's no chick yet, 'only a nice warm egg', so these must be late breeders. Someone asks whether the chick will have a chance, and the answer is a shrug of unknowing.

The wet and the dark and need-to-sleep grumpiness melt away when you are given your first shearwater to hold, shown how to do so carefully so it can't twist its head back and draw blood. How – specific, it feels; how smooth and shaped to its purpose, its feathers silky and elegant, how light and small the body inside them, and how pulsing with life. I have held plenty of dead birds, and live wrens and robins, too, beating themselves against a window; I've cupped a goldcrest in my hand before releasing it and felt the throb of its tiny heart. But this is different. The shearwater will not be controlled, or not for long. It would savage me if it could, to get away. This is being in touch with a living fragment of wild energy. It's an experience not quickly forgotten, perhaps more so because it has not come too easy.

Once the adult birds leave, the nights are quiet, though sometimes I have heard a chick crooning and chuckling to itself underground. With their full set of feathers, the young birds wait for the dark of the moon or a drizzly, overcast night to start the journey on which genes or ancestral memory are prompting them. It is an awesome venture: they must, in a few hours, make their way to the edge of land, avoiding the predators ready to pick them off, find a steepish incline so they can more or less fall into the sea; then they must learn to fly, to swim, to fish, and find their way to South America.

As soon as they are in the water they swim vigorously away from land, making their way south. Still weak fliers, many will be battered to death in storms or blown inland; those which survive fly on alone through the Bay of Biscay, down the coast of Portugal and away from the North Star across to South America. They go off alone, travelling singly, and ringing records show that one or two individuals can make the seven-thousand-mile journey in fifteen or sixteen days. In a few years those that make it will return, often making landfall surprisingly close to the burrow where they were hatched, navigating over vast distances by inherited knowledge and the star-pattern they have learned sitting outside their burrows in late summer.

I never fail to be inspired by the story of these indomitable little birds. But what is most remarkable about those thousands of shearwaters returning year after year, decade after decade, is not the individual achievement, but the physical power transmuted from the green depths into the sky full of whirring wings and homecoming cries. There is an awesome genetic intelligence at work here that must tinge our view of the future with at least a hint of optimism.

Healing

> I would still go there
> if only to await
> the once in a lifetime
> opening of truth's flower
>
> R.S. Thomas, *Island*

Sister Helen Mary, who lived on the island as a solitary for fifteen years, would speak of the island as a thin place, where barriers between dissolve. 'Is it any wonder that people chose this as somewhere to come and die? Its physical shape encourages you to look your last on the world and then to come down the hill to look out into a world beyond.'

It's true there were centuries of pilgrims coming here to die – not to be cured. The stories of a healing well appear only in the nineteenth century and haven't the conviction of other places. The way the island healed was with death, with the resurrection of the soul – lifting it into light, while the body slowly turned back into dust, going beyond dissolution to a glorious amalgamation.

Delivering her letters once, with a bottle of goats' milk from the farm, I commented on how visitors always announce, with a sigh of fulfilment as though they knew it was waiting for them, 'I can feel the silence'. For the island, I said, is never silent. We stood and listened, consciously, to the whisper of moving air, the ceaseless breathing of the sea against rock, the screams of a pair of buzzards tumbling together, a ewe calling its lamb, the squeak of the Carreg gate, the crunch of gravel underfoot, and then Sister turned to me with an air of delivering a revelation: 'But these are the sounds of *Nature*,' she pointed out. 'They are full of spiritual matter.' What visitors notice is the lack of noise: no traffic, no crunch of metal on metal, no throb of machinery or even the faint hum from electricity pylons. What there isn't here comes to seem a positive quality of peace.

At half-past one in the morning, soaked to the thigh and shining a torch on to a hole in the ground, a woman past middle age describes why she is here: 'It's just so amazing

159

– after living in a city all these years, to get out into nature, no traffic, no nothing except natural sounds. I didn't believe there was anywhere like this left.'

'Time is different here,' people say. And one of the first things many weekly visitors do is take off their watches. I'm not convinced that the monks, our monks – who were an Augustinian order anyway – followed St Benedict's divisions of the day into three-hourly parcels for different tasks. You need longer here to get anything done. Perhaps the lighthouse-keepers' three shifts would work better – one each for body, mind and soul.

'Places are holy because people make them so with their prayers,' says the Reverend Evelyn Davies, Vicar of Aberdaron. 'I think it's wonderful the way people learn here to just sit and be – not human doings anymore, but human beings.' I tell her how I am always asked what I find to do all day – how weak it seems to talk about going for walks, looking for shells or watching seals.

Canon Allchin describes Bardsey as a place of precious and irreplaceable gifts. 'It is a door through which we can pass into another world, or better perhaps, through which another world may come to us.' He remarks on the way many of the ancient pilgrimage sites, banned in the Reformation, have recently come to new life, quite spontaneously. 'They seem to be healing places, where people feel released from all sorts of anxieties and fears, where they get a new vision of life. Bardsey is one of them. A holy place which speaks of the present and of the future, no less than of the past, it is a very powerful place *now*.' He pauses. He has known me for a long time; he knows I am not a church-goer. 'For *all* who come,' he adds quietly.

'It's as though it is in some way charged and you just have to be quiet and the island does your praying for you.' The woman who told me this was 'on retreat' from a broken marriage and her job as a probation officer in the Midlands. We were sitting outside the boathouse towards the end of one of summer's hottest days, watching the heron stalking in the shallows. It's a good place for bringing out confidences, that bench. She felt the smallness of the place was good; it was comforting to be somewhere you could walk round in a few hours. I quoted a line of my own from 'Island of Dark Horses': 'Small enough / to see whole, big enough to lose / our own importance' and she nodded in recognition. 'It's a transition place. It helps you to see what really matters.'

In his fortnight's journal published in Welsh as *Enlli* in 1976, R. Gerallt Jones wrote: 'I had glimpsed it through the hurtling waves which beat ferociously on the rocks below St Mary's Well all winter long, looming out of the mist, barely there at all, a mysterious presence. And I had coveted its promise of peace. Now I needed to recover, I was going to Bardsey.' In a few days, he felt better; well enough, in fact, to want to escape: 'I need to know that somewhere else exists, that there is a world elsewhere. And here it can't be done. The sea is all around me, I can't get away. There is only me. I have to live with this me all the time. There's no getting away, no running off into the company of other people . . .' He found himself 'pacing the soft paths like a caged animal', but by the end of his self-imposed solitude he had discovered not only calm but 'resilience' and the island 'seemed spacious, a big enough world, rich and full of minute variety'.

Turn your back on the richness of the world and find another kind; it's an old saw.

The great moral message of our time is that everything in our ecosystem is connected and we have to work our way back to a relationship with the earth that is more than just taking and spoiling. I think of it as a kind of healing of an old wound that none of the organised faiths have been able to more than staunch.

There must have been a time in our development when human beings felt fully part of the natural world. There is a theory that developing mind and self-consciousness – those things that make us modern humans – split us off so that we can rarely achieve the contentment of simply being 'in the moment', a lost sense of wholeness in which Romantic poets and philosophers believed. Goethe, Blake, Coleridge and Wordsworth of course wrote of the visionary moments when they glimpsed what I think of as the basic religious feeling, so old and so deep it might be called an instinct: a sense of oneness so strong it is like being in a giant presence. I have experienced it with clarity twice in my life. It seems to occur when several of the senses are working together, often after vigorous physical effort and more often on mountains than anywhere else – perhaps

under the intoxicating influence of oxygen-rich air breathed deep into the lungs – and is both terrifying and exhilarating.

The first experience was when I was about twelve or thirteen, just the right age for mystical visions, but before I had been influenced by episodes in *The Prelude*. I was walking home from school, carrying two bags of shopping and my satchel and taking the steep way up the rough pasture. It was winter or spring, the elms in the valley were bare, and it was already dusk. Something made me stop and swing round and I thought I saw a huge figure, taller than the trees, stooping above the hen-house in the field behind the neighbours' farm. I knew that it was God, who had created the world and everything in it and who was taking an informed interest in it all – which included me, for I felt attention touch me for a moment, sweep up the hill and beyond, as you might watch cloud-shadow move towards you over a field of green corn, and pass over you. I seemed to scuttle the rest of the way home, a small, cowed creature.

The other was on Bardsey. In the hot dry summer of 1976 fog was a regular nuisance, shrouding the whole island for days at a time. Above, people reported, on the top of the mountain, was clear; you could sunbathe in a world of your own. One afternoon, leaving the baby with Nain for an hour, I climbed energetically through thinning layers of mist and walked along the ridge in blue air, treading a causeway through the clouds, for to right and left, banks of translucent white flexed and quivered like a great swan's wings. Gulls called far below. The grass was so dry it rasped underfoot and I watched thistle-down lifted on a thermal, swirling slowly past. Suddenly a well-shaft opened beside my left hand and I could see straight down to a shower of gold sparks dancing on the water five hundred feet below. I had strayed from the path to the very edge. Even as I looked, I felt warmth like a friendly hand on my shoulder as the sun broke through. I looked up to see it, pale and far away, like a torch at the end of a tunnel, but quickly ripening into what might become a great vague face. Then the sky was full of shifting grey veils once more, with the incandescence fading, moving away. I was encircled, enclosed and distantly through the eddying thick stuff, I heard the fog signal again.

I offer these experiences as evidence of the mind's need for meaning and the power of the imagination to supply it from what is available in the memory banks, although I know that my friends who are lucky enough to have faith will see it as proof of a different kind, and regard me as wilfully blind. The point is that experiences like this, however interpreted, seem significant; they are undoubtedly memorable, recalled across a lifetime crowded with images, and Bardsey is rich in opportunities for them. It is a spiritual resource, a place where at the least people can come to feel recharged, where they can experience delight and wonder, and even a sense of participating in the universe, what Christians would call the Creation – that is, everything we know and can apprehend.

There's another aspect too. Twenty years ago James Lovelock tried to convince us of Gaia, the living planet with the ability to heal herself. I don't believe our ecosystem is alive in any way that we could recognise, but we are beginning to see that nothing on the planet can be separate. We are learning a need for a new relationship with landscape that is not acquisitive – 'sustainable' is the buzz word in both agriculture and tourism. Whether we call them ecotourists or earth pilgrims, Bardsey could have a lot to offer to visitors in the twenty-first century, perhaps in conjunction with a mainland Interpretation Centre so that they arrive with an informed awareness – not needing to ask 'Which way to the birds?' or being disappointed that there is no designated wishing-well.

In Trust

'The whole concept of the island, which until recently was implicit with all manner of promise, is now redolent of loss.'

James Hamilton-Paterson, *Seven-Tenths*

The abandoning of small islands which took place all round Britain's west coast was a result of a profound change in economics and expectations. Once, life was based on the cycle of the seasons – and all most people hoped for was to leave their children a little better off, their lives a little more comfortable. And to hope that, with luck, each year would bring no family catastrophe such as serious illness or a lost harvest. Then came the idea of growth, of expansion.

While Bardsey has always been a separate place, it was not marginal or insular in their present sense of backward, narrow, cut off, or irrelevant. In the twentieth century, isolation came to seem a kind of failure – in Freudian terms, an inability to cope with complex reality – and a frugal way of living as a betrayal of progressive consumerism. The people of St Kilda, Great Blasket, Bardsey, were to be rescued and resettled in decent mainland homes with indoor lavatories and access to 'the kinema'. But while the island represented an economic opportunity, the places of the old community were refilled – in the Twenties and Thirties by farm labourers working their way up to owning land of their own; in the Forties, by several families who came to evade the war. In the last thirty years, since the Bardsey Island Trust took over, most of the homes have to be let on a system of weekly lets marketed as 'The unique Get-away-from-it-all Holiday' (in Welsh, *Ymhell o Sŵn y Byd*, far from the noise of the world). All the land is farmed as one unit, one man walks round with his dog or drives the machines to make the big bales and it's a struggle for a single family to make enough to live on.

In the last half-century, Bardsey has been fortunate in the sort of people it has attracted, more concerned with quality of life than material gain, but there is a 'tipping point' beyond which it is not a viable place to live, even with a salary from outside. One factor is the lack of a school and playmates; another is the dire economic situation for farmers and fishermen. A 2004 radio programme, *Open Country* on Radio 4, focused on lobster-fishing and the interviewer asked Colin about island life. Although the interviewer seemed enchanted by the fact that doors don't need to be locked, she was less enthusiastic about a winter community of only seven adults: 'That's not many people . . . that's not much life, really . . .' Asked if he would like to live there permanently, Colin replied decisively, 'Yes – more and more. I think it offers a lot to young people. It's a real place, and unique. There is no other small island outside Scotland where people are living, *making* a living and being committed to the place in the long term . . . not owning it but looking after it, with a sense of stewardship. You don't find that in very many places any more.

'I enjoy looking around me and seeing the things that exist today and existed through all the history that we can look back to, fifteen hundred years to the old monastery . . . there were guillemots, oystercatchers and peregrines doing just the same as they were today, the same sounds and smells and sights, and that's a nice thing to think, it's satisfying. We're maritime peasants, really, we live off the sea. I'm proud to be a fisherman, and to live in much the same way as people who have gone before, admittedly in a modern version. Yes, we sell our lobsters to France and Spain and we use petrol engines and fibre-glass boats because they're light and strong. But if we had to go back to wooden boats and sails, we could; we could live in much the same kind of way. It's a real life in a real place, it's what life should be, rather than living on concrete and in concrete boxes and juggling virtual money . . .'

The wholesaler explained on air why the price was £5 a kilo less than the previous year (Canadian lobsters, managed and faster-growing, sell for less even after air-freight costs). 'Well, you can't ignore the real world now.' The interviewer sounded almost triumphant. 'Although you might find the life on Bardsey very precious, you can't ever be separate, you can't fight market forces . . .' 'You're just talking economics,' is all Colin could find to say. 'We'll have to fight it, to find other ways . . .'

He has tried. He has diversified, building a large catamaran to carry livestock and machinery and tractors, and now earns as much with his passenger boat as he does from fishing. But he feels this to be demeaning, not a decent way to make a living. 'It's not producing anything. Our world has been reduced to tourism. The island's at its lowest ebb, less useful than it has been for fifteen hundred years. Nobody needs a sanctuary, nobody wants what it can produce – fish, wool, meat. It's easier to make money out of thin air on the internet nowadays than out of land.'

I know what he means. Most of the farmers I know are terribly demoralised, and in Britain at least, their livelihood is hedged about with restrictions and paperwork – and nowhere more so than on Bardsey with all its designations as Site of Special Scientific

Interest, National Nature Reserve, Area of Outstanding Natural Beauty and so on. I try to convince him that enabling people to see seals and dolphins and cormorants is worthwhile – and to make at least a rhetorical link between the pilgrim seeking the place where he may spring into heaven and the modern 'seeker'. I talk about the new hunger for walking, for wild places, mountains, glaciers, moorlands; why not islands? Even if a day trip round the island only makes someone happy, isn't that worthwhile?

Ernest feels 'Bardsey's time will come again.' My argument for tourists as twenty-first century pilgrims having fallen on stony ground, I take a different tack. In the Middle Ages the island stood as a symbol, a summing-up of feelings about the meaning of life. Couldn't it do so again? Not as a haven, a safe place to escape to, but, for example, as a place to show how we might develop a new responsible relationship with the environment. What better place for showing how alternative technology could work? I propose a partnership with CAT at Machynlleth to design a system of sustainable energy with wind-generators, solar and tidal power, and more efficient water collection so that waste could be recycled through reed-beds or even a methane digester – the technology is advancing rapidly-growing crops for bio-fuel. The island could be a challenge and an example. At present we have developed a version of 'compost toilets' with grass clippings, a material to hand on the island and a hundred times better than the chemicals that were brought in by urban tenants in the Fifties and whose main function was to eliminate smell and reassure users. Bardsey is a place for getting back in touch with the senses and the physical, and overcoming squeamishness about our own bodily waste is one example of how it might help us to accept the realities of what we are.

Bardsey can absorb two thousand day visitors a year, according to the Trust's current guidelines. I believe it is a worthwhile way to make a living, and even a privilege, to enable people to see things which we might take for granted – seals lolling about on the rocks like overstuffed sausages, lambs running in gangs before settling down to sleep, dolphins flashing and leaping from dark into light – sights and sounds which bring them delight and wonder. Joy can waken something in an inner world like music; joy is worth it.

I have a feeling that this island is truly 'in the current'; it has always been profoundly related to the world in which it's set and it can mean what we need it to. In the twenty-first century perhaps it can become once again not an isolated rock but a destination – a place apart as it was for the early Christian solitaries but also a valuable spiritual resource, an experience that like a deeply-involving book becomes part of the backdrop of visitors' lives, long after it is left behind.

Autumn Garden

'Keep it! Just keep it as it is.'

Ian Cann, Trust member

Autumn. Early dark.
Glutted on sweetnesses, we
feast our eyes on stars.

Not husks, shed silver petals;
nightwalkers pause, dazzled under
veils of bright dust, slow
scattering of seed broadcast
over the fresh-turned night.
Plough, Polaris, Milky Way:
Genesis made almost manifest
in drifts and stirs of light.

Distance only stars can measure;
ancient peace like stored-up prayer.

Once again, we walk out into the lovely quiet of September – the loud birds gone back to sea, the holidaying visitors and day-trippers returned to the world of gridlock and shopping malls. The island wears its Quaker colours: several shades of grey and brown, a sober green. Bracken is like a russet shawl threadbare in places, pulled tight over the shoulders of the mountain. Autumn skies are lucid and exhilarating, with high big-sailing clouds seamed with gold before sundown: at night the island lies under a riding moon, stretched out open to the stars, full of clear light, holding no secret dark places.

The Michaelmas daisies are out, a straggle of blue stars under the laden apple tree. There are still plenty of vegetables in the garden, partly because I tend to sow them late and because the climate here is so mild. There'll be dwarf beans, perhaps a few snap peas, Calabrese side-shoots, courgettes still flaunting their bright orange flowers, small sweet tomatoes ripening in sunny corners, and the roots – potatoes, carrots, and swede – ready to be cleared. The winter brassicas provide understory cover for late-hatching wrens. I don't like my garden too tidy; tunnels and refuges are important.

Celeriac is just coming into its own by the middle of the month, the feathery tops a rich dark green and spicing finger and thumb with a celery scent. I look forward to eating its knobbly roots, mashed with potatoes to give them a distinctive, nutty taste, or roasted like parsnips. It has more iron even than spinach. The stone walls that I curse for harbouring snails now come in handy for drying onions: I only grow a few, but Dave next door used to bring barrow-loads up from the field, huge red-brown globes and giant clusters of daintier shallots. Digging over the onion bed, I have to be careful with the spade because a robin hops and darts so near, utterly attentive until he's startled by the soft plop of an apple falling into the grass. One day soon we must borrow a ladder to pick the Bramleys on the big old tree against the wall; they are ready, plump and rosy on the sun-warmed side. I met an old man once – in the barber's in Pwllheli, where I'd taken Colin for his first 'proper' haircut – who remembered staying as a boy in this house with his auntie, and how the fruit from this tree filled box after box. So it was well-established even then. I am grateful for it, and for those who planted it and have tended it, for perhaps a hundred years.

Autumn. In our lives, and perhaps that of living on the island too. It's home now to only eight people, and four of those are making plans to be on the mainland for Christmas, leaving only Steve and Jo at the farm with Rachel and Ben, aged thirteen and eleven, facing their first winter here. Such a tiny community hardly merits the name, and yet because we have the island in common and it is so much in our thoughts, those of us who only spend part of the year there bulk up the numbers, psychologically at least. Ernest and Colin will be over every week, weather permitting, bringing mail and supplies and servicing the lighthouse.

October has a quivering note, as if everything were taking a deep breath – the swallows and most of the seals gone, leaving the coves free for mothers and their pups, every bush stirring with small brown migrants, goldcrests and yellow-browed warblers, black redstarts and even, last week, lifted high and flung wide of their usual migration routes by savage east winds – a rubythroat and a red-flanked bluetail from Siberia. There's excitement and expectation up at Cristin, the Bird Observatory: anything could land, now the birds are moving. Walking on the South End sometimes it's possible to hear great flocks unseen overhead, and the wheezy calls of redwing or *tseep-tseep-tseep* of hundreds of sandpipers, tides of birds anxious to reach safety before the long slow slide into winter.

I walked up to Pen Cristin last night to find a signal on the mobile phone. The last of the shearwaters seem to have left; the burrows silent and no scuffling in the gorse bushes. The mainland was dark beyond a sea of hard slate-grey, but the whole western sky a blaze of gold before the red flared into it as the sun sank. At the edge of the lit sky and the blue, the hills of Wicklow were visible, all the way down to the big wedge of Malin Head, like the rim of the world. Violet, vermilion, rose and indigo and gold. The sea was a curve of crystal and the old grey rocks that edge dry land glimmered with trapped light too. As I came back into the house, an image of Wil came into my mind, standing in the doorway where, hour by hour, he used to make his lobster pots, looking out with eyes full of weather and distance.

Jane Strick always used to say, 'As soon as someone's gone round Pen Cristin, we forget all about them.' Because she laughed as she said it, it hurt no more than a joke,

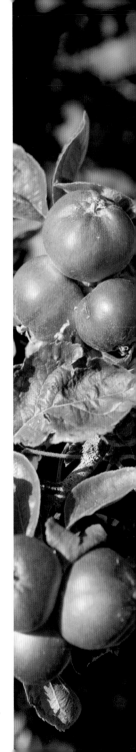

but it is in essence true. What matters on the island is what happens here, with the people who are here now, as in every tribe, every family. But perhaps the island holds whatever a person has put into it: their breath, sweat, tears, laughter and fears and dreams, fragmentary echoes of their stories, even if their bones lie elsewhere.

I am getting ready to leave too, packing up the house for winter and sorting what we need to take and what to leave, putting the garden to bed and making lists of things to bring next year. New horizons beckon for the swallows, already halfway down the world on their epic flights: I wish them warmth and fresh water, and not too many hungry – or, worse – sporty hunters. This, too, is following an ancient pattern: returning from the edge to hunker down in the known winter home. I feel the earth turn and myself ready to lift off for the mainland, for the life of bright interiors, journeys, shopping and friends and new conversations.

'But was it really like that?' I will be asked. 'Is the island really as you say?'

Looking back, for all of us, turns the past into a story with patterns showing clear as a trail through dewy grass – albeit with the awareness of how cleverly memory can cheat. The dead speak in our accounts, although even through diaries and notebooks carefully kept, it is with words we put into their mouths. So this is just my offering, my scattering of words, the best I have at the time, to the spirit of the place and its people.

On a day when the sea seems to have no darkness in it, stretching silver to the horizon, we trundle bags and boxes down to the Cafn. The boat pulls away from the wall and a deep drop opens to the water, across which we stretch hands in farewell. It is always the same, the reluctance to go, even when there are looked-for events waiting. The outboards' blades slice the water, throwing it up under the hull and pushing us along on a plume of white and glittering froth. Round the headland with its sharp juts of stone above the tide's ceaseless wash, past the stacked galleries of pale rock, the empty tenements of the guillemots, the hidden cave of the seals beneath the fallen boulders of Briw Gerrig, and then bouncing out into open water. That whole small world – that focused place, so remarkably living – becomes a featureless grey hump, growing smaller.

And the fierce white rush of the wake carries us back to the mainland.

Closing

Clear evenings in summer we step out
to watch for the green flash, or after sunset
a dark rim beckoning where there was only sea:
Wicklow mountains, Kish, Mizzen Head.

Behind them the horizon
turning to a hearth at bedtime
to warm us with one last flare
and the promise of a fine tomorrow.

But tonight, after a day of rain,
restless steel-grey reaches and the Irish hills
(that had looked like laundry dancing on the line)
suddenly tremble iridescent pearl,

and all perspective shifts

as if the whole world, hushed,
could be afloat on an immense
and breathing stillness, or held
in the lens of a single, shining eye.
Then the heron slaps and shuffles
across the weedy rocks, and the moment's gone:
we're ordinary again, and going dark.

184

acknowledgements

The author and publishers gratefully acknowledge the following sources for writings which are cited.

Chamberlain, Brenda: *The Green Heart*, Oxford, 1958

Chamberlain, Brenda: *Tide-race* Hodder, 1962; Seren, 1996

Chitty, Mary: *The Monks on Ynys Enlli, 500 AD - 1252* (1992)

The Monks on Ynys Enlli 1252-1537 (2000)

Dunn, Douglas: *St Kilda's Parliament* Faber, 1981

Dafydd, Fflur: *Atyniad* Y Lolfa, 2006

Dawkins, Richard: *The God Delusion* Black Swan, 2007

Hamilton-Paterson, James: *Seven-tenths: The Sea and its Thresholds* Hutchinson, 1992

Jones, R. Gerallt: *Enlli / Bardsey* Tern Press, 1976

Jones, R. Gerallt, C.J. Arnold: *Enlli* Gwasg Prifysgol Cymru, 1996

Lockley, Ronald: *Early Morning Island, or a Dish of Sprats* Harrap, 1949; *I Know an Island* Harrap, 1938

Norman MacCaig: 'A Man in Assynt', *Collected Poems* Polygon, 2005

Perrin, Jim: *Spirits of Place,* Gomer, 1997

Pykitt, D, Barber, C: *Journey to Avalon: Final Discovery of King Arthur* Blorenge Books, 1993

Thomas, R.S.: 'Island', *Collected Later Poems* Bloodaxe, 2004

Webb, Harri: 'Enlli', *A Crown for Branwen,* Gomer, 1974

Williams, Bessie: *O Enlli I Gwenlli / Twenty-six Years on Bardsey* Carreg Gwalch, 1996

For Meilyr's poem; *The Oxford Book of Welsh Verse* Oxford University Press, 1962

Quotations (on p. 43, 85,103 and 132) from *Island of Dark Horses*, Christine Evans, *Selected Poems*, Seren, 2003

Thank you to Kim Atkinson for the maps; to Mike Potts, Steven Stansfield and Gawain Davies for photographs of shearwater, seal and stars; and to everyone at Gwasg Gomer for their help and support, especially Mairwen Jones, without whose encouragement this book would not have been written.

1. Tŷ Capel
2. Y Capel/Chapel
3. Abaty/Abbey
4. Nant
5. Hendy
6. Tŷ Newydd
7. Tŷ Nesaf
8. Tŷ Bach
9. Carreg Bach
10. Carreg
11. Plas Bach
12. Cristin
13. Yr Ysgol/School
14. Tŷ Pellaf
15. Rhedynogoch
16. Storws/Boathouse
17. Goleudy/Lighthouse